$\mathcal{N}$o constellation in the night sky has rivaled the Pleiades for its impact upon the mind of man. Artists, poets, scientists, mythographers and prophets alike have not only cited the Pleiades as an inspiration to their work but as a key to understanding Mankind and his/her relationship with the creative principles of existence.

This book is the incredible story of a man who found himself taken to the Pleiades where he was examined and instructed by intelligent life forms who appeared human. The Pleiadians proceeded to give him an education and indoctrination that would enable him to regain his health and attain an unparalleled understanding of electromagnetic science and its role in UFO technology.

Encounter in the Pleiades blends the history of physics and UFOlogy with the personal experiences of Preston Nichols and gives unprecedented insight into the technology of flying saucers and their accompanying phenomena. Never before has the complex subject of UFOs been explained in such a simple language that will be appreciated by the scientist and understood by the layman.

COVER ART: Artist's conception of the flora and fauna of Alderon, a planet in the Pleiades constellation. A Koala is chosen as the totem animal which reigns over the interdimensional aspects of the Pleaides. His pink color reflects an off world pigmentation and also signifies the healing energy of the heart.

ENCOUNTER IN THE PLEIADES:
AN INSIDE LOOK AT UFOS

Written by
Preston B. Nichols
and Peter Moon

SkyBooks
NEW YORK

Encounter In The Pleiades: An Inside Look At UFOs
Copyright © 1996 by Preston B. Nichols and Peter Moon
Print on Demand version, July 2022
Typography and book design by Creative Circle Inc.
Editorial Consultants: Margo Geiger & Althea Carlson

Published by: Sky Books
               Box 769
               Westbury, New York 11590-0104
               websites: *www.skybooksusa.com*
               www.timetraveleducationcenter.com
               email: *skybooks@yahoo.com*

Printed and bound in the United States of America. All rights reserved. No part of this book may be reproduced in any form or by any electronic or mechanical means including information storage and retrieval systems without permission in writing from the publisher, except by a reviewer, who may quote brief passages in a review.

DISCLAIMER The entire content of this book is based upon the experiences and accompanying memories of the authors. The accounts described herein are simply their own freedom of expression of the aforesaid experiences and memories and are protected under the provisions of the First Amendment of the Constitution of the United States of America. The authors have attempted to recount their experiences to the best of their ability. It is up to the reader to evaluate their relative truth. The publisher does not assume responsibility for inaccuracies that may have resulted from induced trauma, misconceptions or human error. Certain names have been withheld or changed to protect the privacy of those concerned. Lastly, nothing in this book should be interpreted to be an attack on the United States Government. The publisher and the authors believe and fully support the United States Government as set forth by the U.S. Constitution.

Library of Congress Cataloging-in-Publication Data

Nichols, Preston B. / Moon, Peter
    Encounter In The Pleiades: An Inside Look At UFOs
by Preston B. Nichols and Peter Moon
    248 pages
    ISBN 978-1-937859-27-5 (print-on-demand version)
    ISBN 0-9631889-3-3 (original 10 digit ISBN)
1. UFOs 2. Pleiades 3. Aliens
Library of Congress Catalog Card Number 95-072820

*This book is dedicated to
Robert Lee Nichols*

CONTENTS

Introduction 9

Part I

Chapter 1 **UFOs, A General History** 13

Chapter 2 **UFO Encounters** 17

Chapter 3 **Aboard a UFO** 21

Chapter 4 **UFO Torpedo Man** 27

Chapter 5 **Technology** 33

Chapter 6 **Twisters & Spinners** 37

Chapter 7 **A Review of Physics** 43

Chapter 8 **The History of Einstein** 47

Chapter 9 **The Speed of Light** 53

Chapter 10 **Warping** 57

Chapter 11 **Contact** 63

Chapter 12 **The Pleiades** 67

Chapter 13 **Aliens** 77

Chapter 14 **Colonization** 81

Chapter 15 **Alien Confederations** 83

Chapter 16 **Abductions** 87

Chapter 17 **Have You Been Abducted?** 97

Chapter 18 **Implants** 101

Chapter 19 **Detecting and Clearing Implants** 107

Chapter 20 **Star Wars** 113

Chapter 21 **Pleiadians to the Rescue** 121

Chapter 22 **The Secret Weapon** 127

Chapter 23 **Returning Home** 131

Part II

Introduction to Part II 139

Chapter 24 **The Psychology of UFOs** 141

Chapter 25 **Angelic Influence** 145

Chapter 26 **Take Me Out of the Ball Game** 147

Chapter 27 **Missing Time** 151

Chapter 28 **Through the Vortex** 157

Chapter 29 **The Secret of Excalibur** 161

Chapter 30 **Missing Links** 169

Chapter 31 **Babalon** 175

Chapter 32 **The Moon** 183

Chapter 33 **Project KOALA** 187

Chapter 34 **Myths of the Pleiades** 193

Chapter 35 **Secrets of the Pleiades** 199

Chapter 36 **Troy, a Pleiadian Outpost** 203

Chapter 37 **All Roads Lead to Rome** 207

Chapter 38 **The Montauk Connection** 213

Chapter 39 **The Pleiades Revealed** 219

Chapter 40 **Lyra & Beyond** 225

Epiloque 229

Appendix A **Antique Saucers** 231

Appendix B **The Particle Accelerator** 233

Glossary 239

Bibliography 243

Introduction

In 1986, Preston Nichols shocked and dismayed the United States intelligence community when he publicly announced to a group of approximately 300 people in Chicago his role in a secret "black project" held on Long Island. Officially known as the Phoenix Project to intelligence and military circles, this activity has been become colloquially known as the Montauk Project (named after the location of the project which was at Montauk, New York) and is the subject of a popular book entitled *The Montauk Project: Experiments in Time* by Preston Nichols with Peter Moon. This book, for which Mr. Nichols is most famous, chronicled major events which involved secret sciences such as weather control and mind control. Allegedly, these developments led to full scale teleportation and materialization of objects which in turn led to the harnessing of time itself.

After publication of *The Montauk Project*, investigation continued in an effort to substantiate such claims. This ultimately resulted in two subsequent books (*Montauk Revisited* and *Pyramids of Montauk*) which corroborate that something of a very irregular nature did occur at Montauk and does so to this day. There are still more people coming forward that will attest to the reality of such a project.

Although Preston's research has been hailed by many and condemned by others, no one can deny that he possesses a mastery of electromagnetic technology and has been involved in covert government research. His professional opinions and advice are still sought after in these circles.

It is one aspect of Preston's connections to the secret sector which is to be the subject of this book: the field of UFOs. *Encounter in the Pleiades: An Inside Look at UFOs* is written in two parts. Part One is by Preston Nichols and concerns his intimate experiences with UFOs, aliens and their technology. It begins with Preston's personal encounters and how he boarded a UFO at the request of the military in an attempt to figure out how the vehicle was engineered. As the book continues, this secret is revealed in a step by step fashion that will leave you with a startling new look at reality and how UFOs function. Certain passages may get a little technical but the language used is non-intimidating and easy to understand. There is plenty of adventure as well.

The second part of this book is by myself, Peter Moon. I have served as Preston's ghost writer for his first three books and this work is our fourth collaboration together. Part Two begins with my own ventures into the paranormal and how these inextricably linked me to Preston Nichols and the UFO phenomena. I conclude by digging into the mythology of the Pleiades and demonstrating how these stars serve as a gateway to anyone trying to understand the phenomena of inner and outer space.

Encounter in the Pleiades: An Inside Look at UFOs will take you on an unprecedented journey in consciousness into the inner realm of the UFO phenomena. After you read this book, you will never look at the subject of flying saucers in quite the same way.

Happy reading.

NOTE: This book contains words that are unfamiliar and unique. Please consult the glossary at the back of the book when you encounter them.

PART 1
by Preston B. Nichols

1
UFOs, A General History

Unidentified Flying Objects or UFOs have been around in different forms ever since the dawn of man. Mysterious flying crafts are mentioned in old Sanskrit manuscripts as well as the Bible. There is Ezekiel's winged fire chariot in the Old Testament and a host of other descriptions if you wish to seek them out in ancient literature. They are nothing new to the experience of mankind, but an understanding as regards their precise nature certainly needs to be improved upon. That is the premise of this book.

Modern day UFOlogy begins in a popular sense in 1947 with Kenneth Arnold's sightings in the northwest and the crash in Roswell, New Mexico. The Roswell crash is particularly well documented and has been reported on in different books and a cable television movie. Although these events were reported on in the common press, earlier sightings were not so well known. In this respect, modern UFOlogy began at least in the 1930s. The earliest sighting I've personally been told of was in 1936. This date, by no coincidence, is when the military was conducting its first experiments with radar. They could for the first time look at an unidentified object in the sky and see by looking at the radar screen that it had actual substance and was not of an illusory nature. This was the first hard scientific proof. At that particular time period,

UFOs were referred to as "flying unknowns" but for some reason the abbreviation "F.U." didn't stick.

Modern rumors of UFO crashes started roughly in 1936 and continued right through World War II until the first documented crash at Roswell in 1947. Since that time period, crashes began to occur at a rate of about one every three or four months. This is why the Air Force began Project Blue Book which was at least a two layered project. The first priority was for the Air Force to seek out and discover all information concerning UFO sightings and crashes. This came under the heading of military intelligence gathering. It vitally concerned the security of the nation. The second priority was to cover up the information and keep it out of the hands of potential enemies. This included keeping it out of the hands of the general public.

In addition to keeping the information out of the public eye for national security reasons, there was another psychological concern. The military thought that a national panic might ensue which could have unknown and possibly disastrous consequences. The 1939 broadcast of *War of the Worlds* proved that masses of people could react quite badly to the news of aliens arriving on planet Earth. In that specific case, people across the state of New Jersey began to barricade, flee and just generally panic when a radio broadcast of H.G. Wells' famous book announced that the Martians had landed. This was neither a prank by the station nor from Orson Wells who narrated the story. The broadcast was fully described beforehand as the reading of a famous book.

There is an even deeper anthropological implication as to why the Government is so concerned and easily upset over the subject of UFOs. If you talk to the average person on the street and ask them where God is, many will point to the sky and answer that "God is up there." If a very advanced culture suddenly arrived in a space ship, large portions of the population would more than likely begin to worship the people in the space ships as angels and believe they were ambassadors from God. With all the different religious sects forming around these beings from the stars, the Government would lose control. All in all, what may have started out as a valid political concern developed into a control issue. Many people would dispute that it was a control issue all along. In any case, publicly elected officials did not make the information known to the public assuming they were even told about it in the first place. The information on UFOs thus became reserved only for a power elite. While this power elite may have various motivations for keeping things secret, it is obvious that leaks have occurred and that disinformation has been circulated so as to keep the public confused and manipulated.

My information comes from my own experiences. I am a professional engineer and understand all aspects of radar. I have known people who grew up in the industry and have heard countless stories. Some of the stories I have heard could be considered leaks, and others are just information passed on by logical deduction. This is the background against which I will relay my story. I will start by telling my own personal experiences with UFOs, beginning with childhood.

2
UFO Encounters

My first paranormal experience was as a child of about five or six years old. I woke up and saw what I believed to be the face of God looking in the doorway at me. This face definitely did not belong to either of my parents. It was very light skinned and was surrounded with long white hair. Although I encountered this face many times, I do not recall any other unusual experiences until I was in my teens. I still do not know if the face I perceived was directly related to my later involvement with UFOs.

It was either in 1961 or 1962, at the age of fifteen or sixteen, that I saw my first UFO. Just prior to that time period, my parents had built me a small red shack in the far corner of our backyard. I was an electronics nut and they wanted to get me and my toys out of the house. As I conducted my experiments, they claimed I was making some of the most bloodcurdling noises they had ever heard. Of course, in those days I had not yet learned how to properly install the negative feedback of an audio amplifier. If it is done incorrectly, there is screaming and howling that sounds like a banshee. It took me a while to understand why. It turned out all I had to do to stop the squealing was to reverse the leads on the output transformers but until I figured that out, the amplifier must have squealed for a week. By building me a shed, my folks let me continue my hobby but at the same time ensured that I was as far away from the house as possible. It was no time before I had the place filled with radio receivers and a couple of old television sets. I even had some test equipment that looked like it belonged in Marconi's laboratory. As I had more test equipment than all my other classmates put together, I figured I was having a good old time as a high school kid.

While tinkering in my lab one night, I couldn't get anything on the radio receivers but a strange humming noise. It kept coming over my radio receivers. Suddenly, I lost all power and the lights went dark. I soon went outside and witnessed a glowing disc shaped object about 200 feet off the ground hovering over my front yard. I estimated the width at fifty feet and the height to be maybe twenty feet. Its color was bright white. All of a sudden and at once, the disc passed right over my head and took off. It moved upward then proceeded to make a few impossible maneuvers before going straight up again. I also noticed that the lights in my house and the entire neighborhood had been blacked out. After a while, the lights came back on.

The next thing I noticed was my mother running out of the house. She was all excited and said, "Did you see that? Did you see that?"

"Sure mom, I saw that." I answered.

"Do you know what that was?" she said.

"I don't know. It looked like a flying saucer to me."

She told me that whatever it was had wiped out the television. I then told her that the radios in my shop had ceased to work as well.

This particular experience was my first "close encounter of the first kind". This is a popular term in UFOlogy that refers to one seeing a UFO. A "close encounter of the second kind" is when you actually see the UFO land while being in the immediate vicinity. A "close encounter of the third kind" is when you are either taken aboard or have communication with aliens. Sometimes an abduction experience is referred to as a "close encounter of the fourth kind".

Chapter Two — UFO Encounters

The UFO sighting in my backyard turned out to be the first of many. Around this general time period (early 1960s), there were a lot of UFO sightings around the area of Islip, the town on Long Island where I grew up and still live to this day. One day, which I recall to be in 1964, I was with a group of kids in high school. The next thing I knew, the school was emptying out with all the students running outside. Out on the ball field behind the school, there was a boomerang shaped craft doing some sort of flying maneuvers. It was very odd and seemed to be only about four feet in diameter. I'm still not sure exactly what it was, but it suddenly took off. That was my second encounter with a UFO.

Sightings occurred frequently when I entered Suffolk Community College in Selden. In fact, students all over campus witnessed UFOs en masse. As I was part of the electrical technology department and had a considerable knowledge of radio, I decided to make it a little more interesting and set up all sorts of spectrum analyzers, radio receivers, and cameras. This did the trick. One night we actually recorded film of UFOs in the sky. They were very clear pictures and anyone who stayed up late at night with me was able to witness the sightings first hand. This was all extra curricular activity and was not treated with security measures of any kind. Consequently, when I came in the next morning to take out the footage, I was disappointed to discover that all the film had been taken from the cameras. It turned out that someone at the college had reported our activity. The result was that we began to be scrutinized by some sort of government authority. When we obtained the pay dirt, they were quick to move in and confiscate our evidence.

Despite the shortcomings of our filming efforts, I did make progress in another area. This period at the college was the first time I had the opportunity to analyze the electromagnetic waves or signatures that these saucer objects generate. What I learned from this research was how to recognize UFOs. These crafts make very distinctive interference on short wave radios and also in the VHF and UHF bands. The spectrum displays usually looked like a hill. I learned to recognize them mainly by the sound that comes out of the speakers while in the AM detection mode when the AGC (Automatic Gain Control) is turned off. They sound like a hum, buzz or a whistle under such conditions. There are also certain patterns in the background noise you can pick up. I became pretty good at recognizing them and now do it primarily by listening through headphones.

All of this was very interesting but was strictly extra curricular to my school work. As events developed, I ended up getting involved in other businesses and projects. Most notable was a rather bizarre antigravity project which ended in commercial failure and was abandoned after pressure was put on me. All in all, it wasn't until about 1974 that I would have another dramatic encounter with a UFO.

3
Aboard a UFO

During most of the 1970s, I was working for a major defense contractor on Long Island. It was in 1974 or '75 when my boss told me that I was selected to be part of a special crew that would be examining some foreign technology located at an unspecified U.S. Air Force base. I figured we were going to look at either Russian or Chinese technology and mentioned that I would be happy to go along. I was then soberly informed that the assignment was not voluntary. I had to go.

There were six of us who boarded an airplane which flew out of Republic Field on Long Island. We flew for a while and then landed. Looking from the air, I figured that we were going to Ohio. As soon as we hit ground and before we could possibly disembark, the pilot taxied along the runway and immediately went into a hangar. We were then shuttled from the plane into the back of a van with no windows. After being driven around for two or three hours, we had no idea where we could possibly be. Eventually, the van stopped and the back doors were opened. We emerged into some sort of underground hangar that was entirely empty. There was no wind or any other descriptive features to this facility, only doors that opened and closed. From one opening, you could see a corridor. We were taken down this corridor and sent to security where we were given a security briefing.

I have said that there were six of us in total. One was my boss but neither he nor the others remember too much of what went on. The briefing was done by Air Force personnel who were easily distinguished by their uniforms. My boss engaged in some rather lengthy dialogues with them. Finally, after being briefed on various security factors, we were taken into another hangar where we saw a disc shaped UFO.

I looked at one of the Air Force personnel and said, "Hey, that's a UFO."

The airman said, "Shhh — we're not supposed to say things like that. It's a foreign aircraft."

He then told us that we were visiting the Foreign Aircraft Technology Group. It was obviously a very clever use of language. The Air Force personnel representing the Foreign Aircraft Technology Group then proceeded to give us a grand tour of the UFO.

From the outside, the craft was silver and looked just like a typical disc shaped flying saucer. It appeared to be about fifty feet in diameter and twenty feet in height. There was also a dome on top that was maybe fifteen feet wide. The entire craft stood on three legs that came out from the bottom. A ramp went up from the ground to a doorway on the edge of the craft.

The most startling aspect of this flying saucer was apparent when I first went aboard. It was absolutely huge inside. The vessel was only fifty feet in diameter, yet we walked in one direction for what seemed to be ten minutes. There was literally hundreds or thousands of feet of space. I couldn't explain it at the time. By today's knowledge, it is apparent that we had entered an artificial reality when boarding the ship. This aspect of a UFO is key to its construction and ability to travel from one location to another. It will be elaborated on later.

Although I have said we were walking through an artificial reality, it was just as real as the environment or room you are sitting in now. The next point of interest I observed was that there were no controls anywhere to be seen. No buttons, levers or knobs. As we walked down the corridor from compartment to compartment, the lights would come on just before we arrived. I looked behind our path and noticed that the lights went off as we left an area. The lighting was very tightly controlled. As we continued to inspect the craft, one of the Air Force crew informed us that the saucer originally contained an odd atmosphere but that it had been "retro-fitted" so that the atmosphere was compatible with human beings.

We eventually came to a compartment that was identified as the control room. The most prominent part of this area were three lounge chairs placed in the front. By lounge chairs, I mean exactly that. They were designed for reclining comfort. A group of smaller chairs were in the back. Our group was then informed that the lounge chairs contained all sorts of coils, wires and other items. It was quite apparent that when a person or creature was reclined in the lounge chair, it was designed to pick the thoughts right out of their head. Readers of *The Montauk Project: Experiments in Time* will note that this technology is hauntingly familiar to that of the Montauk Chair.

On the walls, in front of the lounge chairs, were four view screens. These were also connected to the operators' thought processes. Sitting in the chair, one could call up different maps, star charts, or photographs from outside the craft. Just by thinking the thought, one could view what was outside the craft in any direction.

Behind the view screens there was another small room that had a huge cluster of rock crystals. Coils spiraled around the crystals which were connected at various points by wiring. The walls in this room were nothing but view screens. There were no windows here or in any other portion of the craft.

We were then taken one level above the control area. This was the crew's living quarters. In addition to normal creature comforts, this level contained laboratories and a big medical facility. The laboratories contained large tables possibly used for experimentation upon humans.

Down below the control room, at the very bottom of the saucer, there was one huge room filled with different rock clusters which were all interconnected with wires. Neither myself nor my coworkers recognized anything in the room except for the wiring which was very neat. It appeared to be mostly gold, silver and platinum. We were told that it did not have much copper in it.

Off this bigger "rock room" were four smaller rooms which connected to four hemispherical pods that sat below the center of the ship. Those pods each contained an assortment of what appeared to be antennas. The bottom section of the saucer was insulated from the rest of the craft and was surrounded by a huge coil. This coil was really just a lot of turns of heavy wire and was similar to a degaussing coil used for television sets. The huge coil was connected to the large group of crystals in the central room which appeared to be the central core of energy. This is essentially how the ship was constructed.

From the technology I observed, it was apparent that this craft's drive derived from electromagnetic principles. The four pods contained antennas which generated an electric field. The magnetic field was supplied by the electric coil mentioned above. I will give a more detailed description later on.

As part of our research, the coils on the saucer were activated and we put volt meters on the wires so that we could measure the different voltages. We also observed alternating currents, various wave forms and different frequencies. The craft was levitated about ten to twenty feet off of the hangar floor so that we could do further experimentation and tests. All sorts of antennas and very sophisticated electronic equipment had been set up, and some of it was quite unique. I had never seen it before and still haven't to this day save for this particular instance. There were signature analyzers, spectrum analyzers, and very advanced computers.

Based upon my first hand observations and the theories generated by our group, there had to be some sort of technical reality engineering system in it. What do I mean by reality engineering? Exactly that. I'm referring to the concept of building or creating a reality. If reality is defined as an agreed upon system of perception and interaction that conforms to certain rules, reality engineering refers to changing that system. Or, more importantly, it refers to creating a different system that can interface with the original system or reality.

I know that if I were building a space craft, I wouldn't want to rely on a ship that artificially (by machine) maintains a huge space inside of a small ship. If the machines were to fail, everything could crunch together and perhaps disappear. It could be a nightmare. If I were to do it, I would want a passive system. There would be no electricity and no power. By virtue of the physical shaped structure of the craft I had seen, an alternate reality would have to have been created on the inside. How to accomplish such a feat is another matter entirely and that aspect will be discussed later on.

After working with my engineering team, I concluded there was a single system behind the controls that used the three chairs to pick up commands from the beings in the chairs. The cluster of crystals behind the control room was a computer. The larger cluster of crystals on the lower deck, along with the antenna arrays; all within a coil around the base, I identified as a space-time reality generator. It was a self-contained system and appears to be a simple setup.

After returning to my job on Long Island, there was no mention of the flying saucer field trip by any of my coworkers. It was a confidential matter and was not to be talked about. When I finally did ask my colleagues, they had no recollection. At the same time, I was having memory problems of my own. I was living a buried life that I didn't have full recognition of until years later. It was in this "other" life that I was able to witness another UFO. This one happened to be in the underground facility at Montauk. In my buried life, I was working at both Brookhaven Labs and on the

Montauk Project and saw this craft during a work assignment. This saucer was more oval shaped than the one from Wright-Patterson that I have already described. It had the same screens and chairs but there were also knobs and buttons in addition to a different number of operating systems. I wasn't involved in reverse engineering this craft but was assigned only to help disassemble the different systems as well as the ship itself. The craft came apart in sections which is similar to reports that have circulated about the ships of the gray aliens. In both of these saucers that I witnessed up close, the hull appeared to be an entire unit in itself.

As we disassembled the craft at Montauk, I thought I saw a control system, a computer system and some sort of drive but I was never able to figure out exactly what they were. There was also a radio room of some sort. It is obvious that this vehicle was not being operated under one cohesive engineering system like the one discussed previously. This saucer was never fired up, but I am not sure why. Perhaps they couldn't operate it or didn't know how.

It is obvious to me from what I have personally experienced that the UFO at Wright-Patterson was the most advanced form available and could be considered the Cadillac of flying saucers.* The only thing more advanced would be a purely spiritual vehicle. I will go deeper into the technical aspects of this state-of-the-art flying saucer, but first we will examine my next personal encounter with a UFO.

* See Appendix A for a summary of other types of UFOs that are of a lesser technology.

4
UFO Torpedo Man

My next encounter was in 1989, not too long before I was terminated from employment at the BJM Company. BJM had been contracted by the Government to build a special UHF transmitter and had done a pretty bad job of it. It had been constructed out of very modern avant garde technology that simply didn't work. As I had a reputation for putting together technology for "spook" projects, they decided to turn the job over to me.

After being given the assignment, I picked up the phone immediately and spoke to the customer who told me that he required a pulse modulated transmitter that transmitted at a specific frequency. The information on the exact frequency is still classified. I told him what he needed was a tube transmitter, not a solid state configuration. After we spoke, I went through the warehouse at BJM and picked out an old airport transmitter that would put out about 500 watts of RF (Radio Frequency) in the UHF region. I dusted it off, fixed it up and got it operating to the customer's specifications. It was frequency pulse modulated and ran in the upper UHF band. After it was finished, we took a small helical antenna structure and mounted it on a tripod.

Soon after, I was told to take the transmitter and drive it down to Fort Meade. I signed it out, put it in the back of my Dodge Caravan and made the five hour drive down to

Maryland. Upon arriving at Fort Meade, I was surprised at the lax security. After identifying myself, they simply said that they knew who I was and that I could go down to Hangar 6A or some such designation. Two men from the Government soon joined me. I was told to set up the equipment and wait. One of the guys with me had a walkie-talkie. He got hold of somebody and began to talk into it.

"We're ready," he said.

Guess what I saw next.

A small flying saucer approached until it was right in front of us. As soon as it reached us, it began to turn around. After being so instructed, I turned on the transmitter I brought with me and the saucer suddenly became unstable. It began to wobble and make strange noises.

One of the men then said, "Shut it off. It works."

They then told me to take the transmitter back to the plant at BJM and let it sit there. I went back and told my boss. He said that I could just put it on the back bench in my work space for the time being.

About two months after my trip to Maryland, I kept hearing that the satellite receiver group at BJM was working on some new equipment. According to the reports I was getting, they were tracking UFOs via satellites. What they were actually doing was picking up signals from satellites that had been designed to follow crafts by reference to their electromagnetic signature. This work originally began at a time when the Reagan administration had provided a huge budget for the Strategic Defense Initiative, more popularly known as "Star Wars".

At this particular time period, which I recall to be September 25, 1989, I was told to sign out the transmitter again and take it home. If anything were to go wrong, I was told the equipment was covered by the company's insurance policy. At nine o'clock that same evening, I got a call telling me to take the transmitter to the south end of the William Floyd Parkway at ten o'clock. People would be waiting for me at the end of the parkway and would give me further instructions. At around 9:30, two assistants from work showed up and said they were supposed to accompany me out to the parkway. We all hopped in my van and took off.

Upon arriving at our destination, we found a police barricade. I drove up and said that I had some equipment from BJM and was told to report there. The police said they were expecting me. They told me to go down to the left and check in with the guys at the end of the parking lot. I did so and saw that some of them wore army type military fatigues. Others were in plain clothes or business suits. I was then introduced to a man who told me to put the unit on the back of a jeep. My associates and I then got in the jeep and were driven down the sand dunes to Smith Point, located within Smith Point Park.

When the jeep stopped, we were shown a table that had already been set up for us. To the left of the table and towards the water was a big van with a spinning radar antenna on it. To the right of the table was a big dish with a huge thing in the middle of it that looked like a refrigerator. Normally, this is where the antenna structure would be placed. Towards the water and just ahead of us was a 400 hertz generator which was turned on and humming away.

As I put the transmitter on the table, one of the guys waiting for us pointed out the modulation, power, and RF cables. He said to hook it up and we did. After that, he told us to make sure that everything was working. I then checked out all the stages and everything was operational. Then, he picked up a walkie-talkie and called in to someone.

Next, someone else looked out the back of the nearby van and said, "Turn it on. We're ready for a test."

When I turned on the transmitter, a sort of bluish glow came out of the center of the big dish. It was coming out of the big object that looked like a refrigerator. We could all see a little bit of blue glow reflecting out from the dish and headed towards the sky. Then the man who had called for the test yelled that everything was OK. We were told to stand by and wait.

I believe this testing occurred at approximately 10:30 in the evening. Then, at about 11:00 or 11:15, we heard helicopters in the distance. They were headed towards Moriches Bay from the north. Suddenly, the helicopters began to circle around a point in the sky. A couple of big lights could be seen within the area of sky that the helicopters were circling. The lights, along with the pursuing helicopters, moved south over Moriches Bay. As it came directly over our heads, the crew next to me turned on very powerful lights and we saw a huge wedge shaped UFO. It was triangular and appeared to be at least 300 feet across. It continued to move south until it reached the shore. Then, it made a U-turn and headed back north. By the time it arrived over the water of Moriches Bay, the equipment around me began to hum and buzz. The next thing we saw was the UFO fluttering and wobbling. It made strange whiny noises and then went down. There was a large splash and thud.

No sooner had the UFO crash landed than the man in the van yelled out that the operation was finished. A man next to me said to disconnect the transmitter and put it in the jeep. They wanted us to leave the area as soon as possible and told us to hurry up about it.

My associates and I packed up the equipment and were soon on our way back home. On the return trip, we were trailed by some sort of agents. One of the agents sat in a car in front of my house the entire night. When my two associates left my house, two other agents followed them on their way out. Later that evening, I tried to phone them but my phone line was dead. I went to a neighbor's house and tried to reach them from there. While my neighbor's phone worked fine, I could not get through to my associates. Someone was apparently tampering with their phone lines.

The following day, I went to work and was followed again. I was immediately put through a debriefing procedure and told to forget everything that I saw regarding the UFO incident. By this point, I had already learned how to counter their debriefing procedure. That is why I still remember this incident. The other two employees from the company don't remember anything at all.

Chapter Four — UFO Torpedo Man

The entire incident that occurred is now somewhat famous on Long Island and in the UFO Community. It is known as the Moriches Bay UFO Crash.

What happened afterwards at BJM was really the start of me breaking the "Forget Me Not" security system at BJM. That is what they actually called it. This led to my getting laid off. Some people think that firing me may have backfired on BJM because it gave me ample time to research UFOs as well as Montauk, but this is not necessarily the case. Had I continued to work at BJM with a fully conscious memory, I would possibly have found out even more sensitive information.

The crash I had witnessed at Moriches Bay was undeniable. I had seen something that was very real. I knew the Government was interested in shooting something down, so obviously it wasn't their aircraft. This means that whatever was in the sky was some sort of off world alien technology. The Government must have viewed it as a threat. Also, this pattern of events fit in with what many people in the UFO and defense community have said for years: the Strategic Defense Initiative was not put forth to protect us from the Russians but from alien technology from outer space. President Reagan even spoke about this threat to an assembly at the United Nations. It is all too obvious.

Deciding to study this phenomena a little bit more, I got together with many friends including George Dickson who has extensively studied anthropology and has embraced the UFO phenomena from that perspective. I also consulted John Ford, the founder and president of the Long Island UFO Network. These researchers, along with many others and myself sought to identify what the Moriches Bay crash actually was. Since then, I've become the science consultant to the Long Island UFO Network and have looked into these matters quite deeply. There have been a lot of other crashes and sightings on Long Island, but I do not have specific information on them. That is the province of other investigators.

My own research has centered on the technology of UFOs, i.e. what they are and how they work. This includes how alternate realities are created and how such realities are "moved". This will be covered in the next section of this book.

5
Technology

When I saw the disc shaped saucer at Wright-Patterson, I was most impressed by the fact that there were no apparent controls with which to operate the craft or its various facilities. The only obvious answer to this enigma was that the controls were connected to the three chairs (as said earlier, hauntingly similar to the Montauk Chair) in the control room which were surrounded by four video screens. In other words, these types of ships fly literally by thought. The three pilots (I'm not exactly sure how the work is divided up between them) think of what they want the ship to do. A computer then picks up the thoughts of the pilots and drives the devices which actually power the craft.

When the military began to research these advanced UFOs, there was considerable trouble in figuring them out. The only technology they could refer to was our own technology. This consists of, in no small part, a flight computer and a control deck. Of course, the control deck can be thought to correspond with the chairs. The flight computer has already been identified with the crystals described previously. After that, our technology consists of communications, engines, control flaps and what not. In other words, we have in our aircraft, many diversified systems that the flight computer operates. What has been puzzling in the advanced style UFO is that there is only one system that the computer operates and not a myriad of systems.

The idea that they had a singular homogeneous system makes perfect sense if you consider what the military has done with flight simulator technology. Pilot simulation training began during World War II with John von Neumann's prototype style computer. It has since been developed to the point today where electrodes can be connected to a trainee's head so that he can project his will into the computer in such a manner that his thoughts literally move the dummy aircraft to the left, right, etc. The electrodes attached to the head serve as a computer mouse. As this type of demonstration has been shown on common television, you can bet your bottom dollar that the state of the art technology is far more developed. Of course, those familiar with stealth technology will know immediately what I am talking about. The pilots are trained in this manner which is in fact a virtual reality like setting. Whether a stealth bomber operates exclusively on a pilot's thoughts is an interesting question and one I do not know the answer to at this particular time. But, the stealth bomber is sometimes said to be a "UFO" or to operate just like one.

The next point we will consider in examining the technical basis of UFOs is the incredible gyrations and aerobatics these crafts have been seen to do at a distance. For example, a saucer will be flying along at anywhere from 2,000 to 10,000 miles per hour when all of a sudden the craft will make a ninety degree right angle turn or even a U turn. It is a very well known law of physics that for every action there is going to be an equal opposite reaction. If a UFO were to make such a sharp turn at high speeds, the principles of acceleration and deceleration would come into play. In other words, the pilots and all creatures and loose objects would be slammed against the opposite wall of the ship. Of course, no pilot could experience this trauma under normal circumstances. Some have theorized that space travellers could be suspended in liquid baths that would cushion them against sudden stops or turns, but this line of thinking is far too complex.

Chapter Five — Technology

The system I saw at Wright-Patterson was a device of simplicity. Even so, it took me a while to figure out how this craft actually worked. Although it employed antigravity, it was not an antigravity device by itself. Although it transmitted radio waves, it was not a radio transmitter by itself. Instead, it was a combination of these things, and many more, all put together. The big machine in the bottom of the craft with the pods and antenna structures was an electrogravitic space-time reality generator. In other words, the device was equipped for antigravity maneuvers and was also able to generate its own realities in space and time.

Each of the above two modes of operation have their own particular purposes. When the craft is to glide slowly or hover over a spot, the antigravity method of flight is employed. It is during this mode when you see the actual shape of the craft. What they are doing is controlling the distribution of gravitic currents all around the ship. In this mode, they are not going to make sudden turns because they are subject to the law of inertia.

When a UFO makes a very fast take off, the operators are generating gravitation, but as they progress way beyond the speed of sound, they will move into a mode whereby they will generate their own reality. This is done by creating a reality bubble, not dissimilar to the soloton field that was generated during the Philadelphia Experiment. Once this bubble is made, a craft can move at frightening breakneck speeds. When the UFO goes into impossible flight modes, this is the technology that has been employed.

Once they have generated a "reality bubble" around themselves, they are inside the bubble and everything else is outside. With reference to the bubble itself, they are at rest. Being within the bubble or a still space, their craft can make right angle turns, U-turns or do whatever aerobatics they want it to do. Of course, the only way they can accomplish this is if the mass of the bubble is created to be zero. If there is zero mass, there will be no inertia (inertia = $1/2\ mv^2$ where

mv is mass and v is velocity). In this case, it doesn't matter what the velocity is if the mass is zero, even if v is infinity. If a real zero mass reality can be generated, the operators of such a craft can move that reality in any way they please.

This principle is how most interstellar saucer flights are accomplished. If the flight isn't going to take forever, the travellers need to go beyond the speed of light. In order to accomplish this feat, the reality generated within the bubble must be designed to be relativistic to our reality. In other words, they will go beyond the speed of light with reference to our reality, but in reference to their own reality (within the bubble), they are not. Travelling at super luminal velocities (super light travel), ships can travel from one end of the galaxy to the other in maybe a week of our time. They are moving at a million times the speed of light by engineering a reality wherein the bubble is travelling at just that speed (with reference to our reality). In their reality, they might be moving at $.7c$ or $.9c$ where c refers to the speed of light.

The next point to address is how the artificial bubble reality is created.

6
Twisters & Spinners

In order to convey how an artificial reality is created, it is first necessary to familiarize you with a couple of terms you probably haven't heard before: twister and spinner. These are highly technical terms that are the province of higher mathematics. It is, of course, presumptuous in the extreme to assume that most people reading this book were or are math majors. I will therefore reduce these concepts from the realm of pure mathematical equations into the realm of workable concepts that will enable the reader to understand the logical basis upon which an alternate reality can be formed. Therefore, all technical people should understand that my explanation could suffer here from oversimplification.

Before we go into the more technical discussion of twisters and spinners, I would first like to bring forward to your consciousness the idea of a tornado. In various parts of the world, these are referred to as twisters and sometimes spinners. While this type of weather phenomenon is not identical to the twisters and spinners we will be discussing, it is related and will serve as an easily graspable example to most people. If you look through ordinary books in the library on the subject of tornados, you will find something very interesting. Very strange anomalies have been reported throughout history with regard to this phenomena. After a tornado has whipped through an area, you might find a straw imbedded into a pane of glass or a car imbedded into a steel wall. There are actual reports and pictures of such on file. Under the laws of physics as taught in universities, there is no explanation for this. In such an instance, you have molecules imbedded into other molecules. All of this sounds hauntingly familiar to the reports of sailors being imbedded in the bulkheads of the *USS Eldridge* during the Philadelphia Experiment.

What all of this means is that within the proximity of a tornado, paranormal phenomena can occur which suggests interdimensional activity. L. Frank Baum's *The Wizard of Oz* suggests this very possibility when a tornado takes Dorothy to another world. Writers, particularly science fiction writers, often stumble upon the truth when they start exercising their subconscious.

I hope that all of the above information will serve as a bridge to understanding the more technical aspects of twisters and spinners which we will now engage.

Creating an artificial reality in a flying saucer or in any regard begins with a computer generating what is called a twister. As said previously, this is best conveyed in purely mathematical terms.* A twister, like the entire subject of mathematics, is an abstract concept. It is a dimensionless point that travels in the path of a circle. We can say it exists because its path can be charted in equations. The equations are telling us that some point, although not existing in a solid and consistent manner on the coordinates of this dimension, is moving around and around in a circular pattern. Although it is not observable in this dimension, it is most easily understood if you

---

* Those who are mathematically inclined will be interested to know that the concept of a twister comes from a subject called "Tensor Analysis" which is an extension of calculus. A tensor is like a vector that goes in different dimensions, all at once. You can get an idea of how tensor analysis is used if you can imagine a squashed baseball. Tensor analysis would be used to create a formula for the exact shape of the squashed baseball. However, while the baseball is in the three dimensional world, tensor analysis is not mathematically limited to only three dimensions. Those who want to read more on this subject can consult the books of Roger Penrose. Two of his titles are *Two Spinner Calculus and Relativistic Fields* and *Spinner and Twister Methods in Space Time Geometry.*

Chapter Six — Twisters & Spinners 39

consider it to be adjacent to or in the proximity of this dimension. Although a twister can't be seen, it is a mathematical fact.

Once a twister has been recognized and established to exist, the next step is to tap into the twister. This is done electromagnetically.* When an electromagnetic field is generated, one introduces all sorts of wild and wonderful variables into the situation. Of course, this all depends on the exact nature of the electromagnetic field being employed. The electromagnetism creates a sympathy with the twister (magnetism is a sympathetic reaction) that brings it into this dimension and harnesses it to some extent. As the phantom particle now begins to observably rotate within this dimension, it is elongated into what is called a spinner.**

The first step from a twister to a spinner has been described as the formation of an orbiting electromagnetic wave that forms a torus like pattern. They start with a twister that is formed into an orbiting electromagnetic wave which looks like a torus. Then, the twister is elongated into a rotating cylinder also called a spinner. The cylindrical method is the easiest way I know of to get a spinner going. There are many different types of spinners that can be created depending on your imagination and, more importantly, on the technology you have with which to manipulate them. The standard vortex shape you hear so much about in science fiction and UFOlogy is a conical form of spinner. You can also make a spheroid spinner by connecting the two ends of a rotating cylinder. The more imaginative can envision other shapes such as a whipsoid (an elongated spinner with a random

---

* By definition, this operation would not absolutely have to be done electromagnetically. It could conceivably be done with any form of energy that would do the trick.

** For mathematicians, a twister is first generated with a function in the x, y plane. To stretch it into a spinner, you distort the x, y function with a z function. If you are working with an imaginary plane, you replace the x, y, z coordinates with I, J, K as is customary in math. A twister and then spinner can be generated out of an electromagnetic field which can be accomplished with a Delta-T antenna. This is a three dimensional octahedronal antenna with coils placed around the entire structure giving you an X, Y and Z axis. By modulating the x and y fields in a Delta-T, you can make the spinner take on different forms.

path that follows the pattern of a whip) or other complex patterns.

At this point, it is very important to mention something with regard to the spheroid shape mentioned above. The physical Earth is a spheroid. If you consider that the physical Earth itself is literally constructed upon a series of energy grids that conform to spirals of energy, one can visualize that the Earth itself was initially created out of a spinner.* This line of thinking implies that someone engineered the Earth into reality. Was it God or an alien manipulator? It brings to mind all sorts of intriguing questions which are not the subject of the discussion at hand.

The idea of the Earth having formed as a spinner also gives us an alternative view to the Big Bang Theory of the Universe. The Big Bang Theory says that we all started from one point of explosion at the center of the universe. What I might call the Spinner Theory, suggests that heavenly bodies may have formed as the result of a cosmic reality engineer creating an electromagnetic field that the planet is based upon. The Big Bang Theory is correct to the degree it states there is a spiraling out from the center of the known universe, but its primary aim as used by the scientific establishment seems to be to sell us on the idea that we are all physical matter anyway. In other words, it is more propaganda. Of course, good propaganda is based upon as much truth as possible.

There are a whole series of programs and patterns that can be programmed into twisters and spinners. Once power is put into them as well, you can generate a spatial warp. Out of that warp, a reality is engineered. This is done through radio transmission. At Montauk, we used a large transmitter along with a Delta-T (octahedron shaped) antenna to accomplish this same end. While I have personally experimented with impressing thought forms into the Delta-T antenna, I have not made anything solid or physical with it. That would require considerable power. Although radio transmission was definitely used in the UFO I was aboard at Wright-Patterson,

---

* As the center of one of these spinners is a void, this concept also conforms to the idea of a hollow Earth.

Chapter Six — Twisters & Spinners

I was not able to identify any sort of specific radio transmitter that I was even slightly familiar with.

It was stated in *The Montauk Project: Experiments in Time* that the window frequency to the human consciousness is 400 to 450 Megahertz. What this means is that this particular frequency will carry information or ideas which we term consciousness. It is not open to question that radio and television carry words and ideas. The 400-450 Mhz just happens to be how you get an idea into someone's head. How well this is accomplished and how forceful it is depends on various factors. The idea is that a properly educated and trained consciousness can project to another on this frequency. If the technology (which requires amplification of thoughts as well as a myriad of other factors) of the operators can make their ideas stick, you will have a whole series of circumstances that are consistently present: in other words, a reality. This area is actually an entirely different and very huge subject which is properly labeled "reality engineering".

To summarize, a twister has no dimension. It is generated from a computer, encoded and then spread into a spinner. This starts out as a rotating cylinder which is in turn shaped into whatever form is desired by the operators. This creates a spatial warp around the specified area targeted. For practical purposes, it can be considered like a vacuum. In keeping with the principle that nature abhors a vacuum, the spatial warp serves as a backdrop for a new reality which is in essence a series of thought forms being transmitted at a frequency of 400-450 Mhz.

This gives you a bubble reality. Before we discuss how this bubble reality can interface with other realities, it is appropriate to give a brief history on how the subject of physics developed.

NOTE: Research and compilation for Chapters 6-10 has been assisted by Peter Moon.

7
A Review of Physics

Before Isaac Newton came along and began to codify the first phase of what we know as modern physics, the world was a very different place. Alchemy was the order of the day when it came to learning the secrets of the universe. Alchemy dealt with the qualitative as opposed to the quantitative nature of matter. This means that it was broken down into the four elements of earth, air, water and fire. This subject further delved into the sympathies or correspondences between material objects and other forces. In all due respects, this was the study of magic.

Common history books on the sciences will sometimes portray alchemy as a subject that was based upon infantile and naive observations yet paved the way for the investigation that would result in modern science. Almost always, alchemy is portrayed in a ludicrous manner. It will also say that the goal of alchemy was the transmutation of metals into gold. While there is definite truth in the last statement, it is misleading. Alchemy in its highest form was concerned with the transmutation of consciousness. Physical objects were considered a manifestation of consciousness and were not thought of as independent or objective objects in their own right. Of course, if one could change consciousness and was very good at it, one could also change metal into gold.

In other words, alchemy is another way of saying metaphysics. Both these words have their own specific connotations, but they are both concerned with the idea of forces that are superior to the common physical world.

It was out of this background that modern physics arose. If you look at some of the old alchemical writings, you will discover they were written in code. In other words, a modern historian investigating the subject wouldn't have a clue. The true secrets of alchemy were relegated to the secret societies of the day.

Modern science got its first shot in the arm when Isaac Newton discovered and formulated the laws of gravity and motion. These laws are still with us today for the most part as they are of undeniable practical use. If you study his entire career, you will discover that Newton was a brilliant man and that his work was nothing short of astounding. He claimed to be inspired from a higher source. The major flaw in his work was that he considered objects to be at rest. For practical use, his idea was workable. Newton's laws worked and helped to launch the mechanical age.

The next major event in the history of science occurred in 1887 with the famous Michaelson-Morely experiment. This experiment was considered a major and astonishing failure yet it sent shock waves through the scientific community that are still with us today. Albert Michaelson, a physics professor, and Edward Morley, a chemistry professor, sought to prove the existence of a substance called the "aether" which was believed to fill all of space and was also thought to serve as the substance along which light waves travelled. Virtually all scientists of the day believed in the concept of the aether. It was a unified field of sorts although it really couldn't be called such as there were too many unknowns in the popular physics of that day.

The concept of the aether began with the alchemists of old. They conceived of a medium that embraced the entirety of existence(s). To them, the aether was unlimited and not only served normal space but the subtle and spiritual aspects of existence as well. It was the very fabric of existence itself. When the influence of Newtonian physics began to place the emphasis on strictly physical concerns, the more noble aspects of the aether were lost. As physics developed, the concept of the aether was used to describe the medium through which light and electromagnetic waves travelled. The logic employed was that if sound made waves in the air and that if motion in the water made ripples or waves, then light should consist of waves in a similar medium. Further, if there were such an aether, it was readily assumed that light would be slowed against an aether "wind" as it travelled. Thus, the aether could be measured and proven to exist.

Michaelson and Morley set out to prove whether the aether existed by emitting two beams of light from a single light source and measuring the difference it took the two beams to return to the original spot. This was done with mirrors in such a manner as to replicate one beam moving with the orbit of the Earth while the other beam would be going in a counter orbital direction. The theory at the time was that the Earth in orbit was moving along a "wind" (the wind of the aether) or momentum. Michaelson and Morley discovered to their surprise and dismay that the two beams of light returned to the source in identical time periods. This meant that the aether had no visible signs of evidence. It didn't exist! The news of this experiment rocked the scientific world of the day and for all practical purposes, the idea of the aether was abandoned and eventually highly ridiculed and scoffed at with much disdain.

Of course, this entire assumption suggests that the aether is a measurable force. Just because it was not measurable, it was denounced as scientists are quick to dismiss anything they can't measure. None of this actually meant that there was no aether. It just meant that there was nothing found that met with their preconceived notions.

Many of you in the reading audience may have never heard about the Michaelson-Morley experiment but any scientist knows it very well. What is significant about it is that it was one of the biggest PR events in the history of modern science and has been hailed as a major breakthrough. It changed the entire direction of scientific thought and at the same time buried the idea of the aether. At the same time, in the collective unconscious, it served to bury the idea of the alchemists' aether too.

What is particularly interesting about the Michaelson-Morely experiment is that breakthroughs in science generally result in tremendous discoveries and solutions to all sorts of problems. It is hard to think of any technological advances that resulted directly from this experiment. Even Albert Einstein, who was the next scientific celebrity to leave his mark on the scene, said it had no significant impact on his work. Before we examine his work, we will first take a look at some interesting aspects of his personal history that have been generally overlooked.

8
The History of Einstein

Albert Einstein was a most curious figure. Heralded as one of the most brilliant minds of history, he was renowned for not being able to find his own house in Princeton. During his stay at Cal Tech, he routinely depended on others to tell him how to get to work. One story even has him falling down a manhole as he strolled along a walkway. Before we examine his contributions to science, we will first give an historical account of key points in his background that are often overlooked.

In the general public's mind, Albert Einstein is without a doubt the most famous figure in the history of physics. Most people have not heard the story that he studied in Zurich under one Hermann Minkowski who taught the Unified Field Theory. Minkowski is mentioned in many physics books as Einstein's teacher and is even credited as playing a pivotal role in Einstein's ideas. Minkowski's role is severely understated.

The information about Minkowski teaching the Unified Field Theory was told to Peter Moon by Dr. Jean Keating, a medical doctor from Delaware. According to his information, Einstein was sent to the Swiss Federal Polytechnic School (now known as the Eidgenussische Technische Hochschule or ETH for short) by the Rothschild banking consortium. When Einstein failed the entrance exams, Rothschild pulled strings to get Einstein admitted. In the book *Einstein, His Life and Times* by R.W. Clark, on page 35 Minkowski describes Einstein as a "lazy dog" who "never bothered about maths at all".

When Einstein graduated in 1900, he found a job in the Swiss Patent Office in Berne, Switzerland. It is while in this position that he produced his first major scientific theory. Although some people have claimed this was an unlikely job for someone of his talents, one sees a pattern being set. Einstein is sponsored by a vested interest (the Rothschilds); he gets a job in the patent office and gains access to the cutting edge scientific discoveries of the day. He then produces theories that are acclaimed by the press with accolades no other physicist has received before or since. Of course, the Rothschilds controlled the press.

There is no contention here that Einstein is incorrect but there is a suspicious pattern in the way physics has been rendered to the general public. Einstein was heralded every step of the way. Although his findings leave the world of physics wide open, his ideas were portrayed so as to reinforce our limitations. Again, we are forced to look at Einstein's impact on world technology. The most immediate impact was the atom bomb which would be followed by nuclear power several years later. This is a controversial field to say the least.

The nuts and bolts theory of the atom bomb project were actually provided by John von Neumann, but it was Einstein's backing of the project (which he later regretted) and letter to Roosevelt which sold the president on its possibility. Einstein's theories helped paved the way and he is sometimes credited with putting it within reach. Although a tremendous amount of technology has sprouted out of the U.S. space program, Einstein's impact on that was virtually nil. A magician named Jack Parsons (who believed in the principles of alchemy) was primarily responsible for the development of the solid fuel rocket and the consequent success in getting mankind into outer space. There is considerable irony in all of this. Einstein is portrayed as a gentle humanitarian while Parsons has been cast as a devil worshiper.

Chapter Eight — The History of Einstein

The fact that Einstein had difficulty finding his way to familiar locations is not the only piece of evidence to suggest he was programmed. There is a very interesting mention of Einstein in the book *The Wind and Beyond* which is the autobiography of Theodore von Karman. A friend of John von Neumann (both men were from Hungary), Von Karman cofounded the Jet Propulsion Laboratory with Jack Parsons, Frank Malina and Ed Foreman. He was the fatherly figure of the group and was considered one of the top scientists in the United States. In his autobiography, Von Karman begins Chapter 33 with a very puzzling statement. He mentions entering a sanitarium at Lake George, New York, in order to convalesce from a serious intestinal operation. Since when does one need to convalesce in a nut house?

Von Karman then mentions that after falling ill with carcinoma, he was "ordered" to a private clinic in New York City where a famous German surgeon by the name of Dr. Nissen operated on him. I will quote from page 267 of his book:

"He (Nissen) said later that he had saved my life, but I saw only that I was left with a hernia after the operation. I told the doctor that if an aircraft mechanic were to make a weld of metal similar to the junction he had made in my intestines he would be fired. But Dr. Nissen had no sense of humor. He reported to my worried sister that the shock of the operation must have disturbed my mind. My only consolation was that, two months later, he operated on Albert Einstein and also left him with a hernia."

The above quote speaks for itself, but there is an even more bizarre aspect to this story. Those of you who have read *The Montauk Project* and *Montauk Revisited* may remember the character I called Dr. Rinehart. He had claimed to me that he was John von Neumann and had been put into a witness relocation program. When I introduced him to Peter Moon in September of 1993, Peter was struck by the fact that this man has an enormous bulge between his legs which I have been told was the result of a botched hernia operation. He has lived with it for an

Einstein's Unified Field Work Documented

On a research trip to the public library, I stumbled upon an interesting article. Before I got to the material I was looking for, I noticed a bright yellow band on the binding of a book. "1943" appeared in black letters. It was a summary of *Time* magazine articles from 1943. I picked it up and looked for news releases from August of that year, the alleged date of the Philadelphia Experiment. To my surprise, there was an article on Albert Einstein and the Institute of Advanced Study where the Philadelphia Experiment was reportedly hatched. It was dated August 9, 1943 and you can find it in that issue of *Time* magazine. The article was entitled "Cooking With Water" and read as follows:

"Princeton, NJ has one school whose teachers do not count on teaching their students a single solitary fact. It is the ten-year-old Institute for Advanced Study. Its faculty of 16 includes Albert Einstein. Its 28 students do post-postgraduate research, are so expert in their fields that they are presumably aware of all the known facts involved. All that the Institute's teachers hope to do is to broaden and deepen their students' points of view toward their subjects by joint approaches from new angles. The students hear few formal lectures, take no examinations, get no degrees."

"Last week, however, many were hard at work in the kind of abstruse study which used to be a European specialty. Albert Einstein himself was busy trying to unify certain theories of gravitational and electrical forces in order to solve some complex mathematico-physical problems for the U.S. Navy. His aureole of white hair droops in summer's heat, a string upholds his cheap blue denim pants. Says he: "Here we cook with water." Interpreted a colleague: "We perform no miracles." A current item of Einsteiniana titillating the Institute: on one of his blackboards bearing a brain-taxing mathematical equation, the charwoman found the word "Erase." On another blackboard, marked "Do not erase," was blazoned the formula 2+2=4."

The handwriting was on the wall. What is also amusing about this article is that Einstein is described as keeping up his pants with a string. For those of you who remember Dr. Rinehart (the man mentioned in *Montauk Revisited* who Preston believes is John von Neumann), I didn't mention that he also kept his cheap pants up with a rope. Do unified field scientists have some secret taboo against wearing belts? Does the combination of metal and leather affect their thinking process? Or better yet, does wearing ropes give them a strange kundalini power? Probably, the very nature of their thinking process causes them to disregard their personal appearance. But, it should be mentioned that both von Neumann and Einstein have been pictured in their early days as wearing suits and looking fashionable for the times. One has to seriously wonder if the blatant disregard for their self-image is related to some sort of programming. ■

The above article by Peter Moon is reprinted in full from *The Montauk Pulse*, Spring 1994, Issue No. 6.

amazing twelve years.

The above circumstantial evidence suggests these men were manipulated or programmed. One person has even suggested that their testes or parts thereof were extracted in an attempt to reproduce their sperm. The theory behind this is that brilliant minds could be produced from artificial insemination. That it was a German doctor only adds to the intrigue.

Amazing as it may sound, there is no intention here to knock any of Einstein's discoveries and theorems. But it should be pointed out that a media spin was put on his work ever since the beginning of his public career. Nikola Tesla's work was much more remarkable and practical in nature yet he was given nowhere near the acclaim of Albert Einstein.

With Einstein's work, there is not much wrong with what he had to say, but there are a tremendous amount of things he did not say. It was rumored since the days of the Philadelphia Experiment that Einstein had completed the Unified Field Theory and that it was kept secret by the military. The article from *Time* magazine on the preceding pages substantiates these claims.

This brief overview of Einstein's history will hopefully enable everyone to consider his work in a new light (no pun intended). We will now continue our review of physics beginning with his work.

9
The Speed of Light

After the Michaelson-Morley experiment of 1887, the next big news to shake the world of physics was Einstein's Special Theory of Relativity which was first made public in 1905.

In Chapter 5, I said the reality generated within a bubble reality must be designed to be relativistic to our reality. In other words, the travellers in the bubble will go beyond the speed of light with reference to our reality, but in reference to their own reality (within the bubble), they are not. This is a bit of an oversimplification because according to Einstein's Special Theory of Relativity, nothing can travel faster than 186,000 miles per second (the speed of light). Einstein's theory includes the principle that no means of energy whatsoever can move faster than c, the speed of light. Therefore, if the travellers within a saucer's bubble reality were moving at a reasonable speed in their own reality, but were moving faster than the speed of light with reference to our reality, there has to be some accountability for the fact that energy in our reality cannot go faster than c.

All of this, of course, presents limitations with consequent problems of theory. Before we discuss this further, it is appropriate to give a brief overview of some key developments in the history of physics.

When Einstein came along and introduced us to the Special Theory of Relativity, he said that the speed of light is constant and independent of the motion of the light source. In other words, no matter what observation point we are in, light moves at a constant speed.

This is a most interesting statement. What is even more interesting is what Einstein does not say. He does not tell us about the speed of light after it is passed through a prism. If you put a light through a prism, it will display a spectrum that breaks down light into different colors with accompanying different speeds. The lowest frequencies have faster speeds while the higher frequencies have slower speeds. At first glance, you might think that the speed of light is not a constant speed and that Einstein was wrong.

Well, not exactly. If you look at the world around you, you will again possibly think Einstein is wrong because the world is full of different and beautiful colors that are moving at different speeds. The light Einstein is referring to in his Special Theory of Relativity is not the same light you see in the every day world. He is talking about light in an absolute vacuum. If you were to measure any specific form of light you encounter in your travels, it could only approach the speed of light. Even outer space is not a perfect vacuum and the light therein could only come approximately close to the speed of light. Actually, laboratory vacuums can do better than outer space. Although lab vacuums are technically not absolute vacuums either, they can come pretty close.

All of this tells us that the light Einstein is talking about is something that we do not have a reference for in normal experience. Of course, the colors we see in life are a distortion of true light. Most of our light is emitted from the heat of the sun which is distorted through our atmosphere.

While some scientists of the day stated that light consisted of continuous waves, Einstein's further research led him to believe that light consisted of a continuous stream of particles which he termed photons. Scientists have since hotly debated whether light consists of waves or particles. This is an intriguing area of research in itself and some people even meditate on the exact point where a wave becomes a particle with consequent transcendental experiences.

In a pure vacuum, photons will manifest as a wave of pure energy. They do not manifest as particles. This is pure light as Einstein defined it in his Special Theory of Relativity. But, when light is subjected to a magnetic field, it changes and breaks down into particles or photons. In such a state, it is no longer **c**. In other words, it is no longer the same light that moves at a constant speed.

In this sense, it can be said that magnetism is an intrinsic factor in the creation of matter, if not the primary factor. It is also noteworthy that everything you see in the world around you is magnetized light which is in reality a distortion of pure light (or *c*).

The idea that magnetizing pure light turns this particular type of energy into particles is very important. The corollary of that statement is that if you demagnetize light, you are going to have pure light provided you are in a vacuum.

Next, let us consider what happened during the Philadelphia Experiment. There, the Navy had extensive degaussing coils placed around the hull of the ship. They were attempting to demagnetize the hull so that the ship would not trip underwater mines (which were designed to explode when coming into the magnetic range of the metal hull). As there was also a soloton field created around the ship, this served as the vacuum or bubble reality. When the ship was demagnetized, the particles of matter became waves and the ship was gone. The consequent weirdness that ensued is another matter entirely.

The general principle is that if you demagnetize matter (which can be done through the use of coils as was done in the Philadelphia Experiment and as described in the UFO I went aboard), you are converting it into pure light which is something that cannot be experienced in every day reality. It is a pure energy and could even be considered a realm unto itself.

Once light or matter has been demagnetized and turned into pure waves, it has to be manipulated or controlled in some fashion if it is to be used. This is where the frequency of 435 Mhz comes into play. As was said earlier, 400-450 Mhz is the window to human consciousness. It is also a truism that there is a noise peak emanating from the Milky Way at 435 Mhz (the stars emanate this frequency). Everything in our reality is believed to exist on this undercurrent of reality. In other words, it appears that 435 Mhz is the background reality of our universe.* If light is demagnetized and in wave form, transmissions can be inserted into it that will reassemble the light. If one can project consciousness into the vacuum that has been demagnetized, the wave form has been given an advice or program command which will result in a materialization at some point. There are various ways one can imagine this to be done. In this sense, light from a pure vacuum is demagnetized and exists in a void. If one sends a transmission into that void at 435 Mhz, a thought form is created that reassembles the light into a reality.

The important point is that this is the general principle on how space travel, an allegedly impossible task, can be accomplished.

* There is no question that 435 Mhz not only accesses consciousness but emanates from our galaxy. Unfortunately, there is no available information on this frequency that I am currently aware of. It is still a mystery, and we hope that someone in the reading audience can supply further information. It is possible that information on this frequency is one of the most closely guarded secrets in our universe. If it is indeed the background to our reality, it is quite possible that knowledge of this information would enable one to literally change reality before our very eyes. Technical people should consult the definition of "435 Mhz" provided in the glossary of this book.

10
Warping

Now that we have examined some of Einstein's statements from a fresh perspective, lets take a look at what he actually said in his Theory of Relativity (as taken from *Webster's New World Dictionary*):

1) There is no observable absolute motion, only relative motion.
2) The velocity of light is constant and not dependent on the motion of the source.
3) No energy can be transmitted at a velocity greater than that of light.
4) The mass of a body in motion is a function of the energy content and varies with the velocity.
5) Matter and energy are equivalent.
6) Time is relative.
7) Space and time are interdependent and form a four-dimensional continuum.
8) The presence of matter results in a "warping" of   the space-time continuum, so that a body in motion passing nearby will describe a curve, this being the effect known as gravitation, as evidenced by the deflection of light rays passing through a gravitational field.

Einstein is telling us that there is a fourth dimension which consists of time and space. It does not take a genius to realize that if "matter results in a warping of the space-time continuum" that everything in our world is a distortion of a more basic reality (the fourth dimension). This only backs up what I've been saying, but as was said earlier, a negative media spin has been done with most of his work.

If you magnetize pure light, it will bend and distort. It is interesting to note that the word magnet actually derives from the root "magus" which means magician or practitioner of magic. The alchemical analogies and correspondences never seem to leave us if we bother to look for them. Our three dimensional universe, as it appears to us, is actually magnetized light.

In the previous chapter, we accepted that one could not only convert matter to energy but to a higher form of energy than is actually experienced in this universe: light (demagnetized light, to be more specific). We were concerned with travelling at the speed of light or exceeding it. This requires the warping of reality as we know it. Actually, the fourth dimensional reality had to have been warped in order to get us into our current condition.

For practical purposes, a warp means that the bubble travellers have gone from one area of the universe to another by "cheating" because the energy could not be displaced without appearing somewhere else. Or, it means that a warp (tunnel or vortex) opened up and the bubble travellers went through it and that no displacement of energy took place.

The definition of warp is to twist, bend or distort. Obviously, one has to twist or bend space to accomplish this. Because time is intrinsically and mathematically connected to space, one needs to warp space and time. In order to understand how this could conceivably take place, we need to continue our review of the history of physics.

As science developed in the early part of the twentieth century, Einstein's discovery of photons or particles of light helped lead to a new subject which is now called

Quantum Mechanics. This subject deals with the "quanta" that the known nuclear particles (protons, neutrons, electrons, etc.) consist of. Although Einstein never fully embraced this field, there were plenty of notable scientists who did. John von Neumann was at the forefront and we can learn from one of his statements. He said that the sheer volume of mathematical papers of the day made it entirely impossible to read and understand them all. He estimated the most one could grasp was ten percent of what was out there. Obviously, there was more theoretical science being developed than one could even comprehend, scientist or not.

Quantum Mechanics is primarily a theoretical subject which seeks to discover and explain the tiniest particles of existence. There are many who accept it and some who do not. Those physicists who are called "purists" when it comes to the hard physical sciences often refute the general and specific theories that have been offered in the quantum world. While they sometimes have very valid points, much of the criticism of quantum physics is by those who are given to rant and rave and have an agenda of their own.

The subject of Quantum Mechanics becomes very helpful in trying to understand what a warp is; especially when we consider one of the tiny particles of physics: the quark. A quark refers to a subatomic particle. In other words, if you break down an atom into the particles that make it up, you will find they are made up of quarks. Of course, modern quantum physics has discovered all sorts of different names for particles that accompany or make up quarks but an explanation of those becomes rather complex in a work of this sort. Those interested can read up on it. The main point of a quark in this discussion is that experimental observation of these particles have demonstrated that they are not stable in reference to time.

To make this clearer, the particles that make up our reality are not stable in our reality. They will appear and then disappear. If we want to consider quarks to be waves of energy, whereby the particle is considered to be the manifestation of a wave, that is fine. But that wave of energy is not entirely traceable in terms of normal electromagnetic phenomena in this reality. In any case, a quark as well as other subatomic particles are referenced to some other reality. It they were not, they would appear consistently within our reality. If the quark is a wave, then such a wave is emanating from another reality. The carrier is not found in our reality (according to current measurement standards) but would obviously be bridging to our reality because it can be partially perceived. That it can bridge to our reality suggests that it can be traced. We just haven't discovered the precise means to do so.

The quark is therefore demonstrably interfacing with another reality and doing it on a regular basis. The idea of the quark has been introduced so you will understand that there is a bridge between this reality and another one. Some theoreticians refer to these other realities as chaos. We will deal with that aspect in just a bit.

When a UFO moves beyond the speed of light from one location to another in such a manner so as to apparently violate Einstein's Theory of Relativity, it is warping or bridging to another reality and then reentering this one. Of course, Einstein never said that you couldn't go outside of our reality and thereby exceed the speed of light. He just said that you cannot go beyond the speed of light within any particular reference frame.

When a reality bubble is created within a UFO to protect the creatures aboard and maintain their normal reality, the rest of the ship can travel at high speeds but ultimately will have to warp out of this reality if it is going to move to another star system with any reasonable speed. It does so by bridging to another reality and then coming back to this one, not unlike the quark.

Earlier, I referred to chaos and this is very important when we consider the subject of UFOs. It is also important when we consider the subject of quantum mechanics. As that subject developed, it became obvious that no matter how intriguing the theories, none of them offered scientists information by which they could absolutely predict the behavior of subatomic particles. You can understand how lack of prediction can drive a scientist crazy and understandably so when you consider that their profession is based upon predicting results. Instead, quantum mechanics developed along the lines of probability. In other words, quantum physicists would predict behavior in terms of statistical probability based upon observation. This is like watching a baseball player hit for a certain batting average. No matter what his average or the circumstances, his next turn at bat is entirely unpredictable.

Einstein parted company with the quantum physicists when he made his famous statement: "God does not play dice with the universe". He, as well as many others, believed that quantum physics was only describing phenomena that could ultimately be predicted with supreme cause and effect. Quantum Mechanics as it stood was only an incomplete science that could predict probabilities. It was rejected because it was not absolutely precise beyond the shadow of a doubt.

The probabilities the quantum physicists were spouting were really opening the door to a subject that made traditional scientists very uncomfortable: chaos! Somewhat humorously, chaos could be considered the "shadow" beyond the doubt.

An entire new subject called Chaos Theory has since developed which seeks to track and categorize phenomena hitherto unknown. For example, random matter in nature is broken down into repeating patterns that reveal forms of geometric order that were previously unsuspected. No matter the various advances that are made and the symmetries and order that are found, further chaotic and unpredictable factors can always be discovered in both regular and biological matter. This could also be linked to the radical factor in evolution.

Chaos Theory tells us that basically anything you can conceive of does exist or will exist. It is an unlimited concept of existence. This totally embraces our current times where all sorts of paranormal and anomalous phenomena are beginning to get recognition. It only fits that UFOs would be opening the doors to chaos.

The word chaos itself has been given a somewhat sinister reputation, but the concept is largely misunderstood. The concept itself was known by the ancients and is referred to as Chaos Magic in popular occult literature. Author Peter L. Carroll defines chaos as the force that animates all events in the cosmos. He says that while others may refer to this phenomena as God or the Tao, he prefers to call it "Chaos" because this term is "virtually meaningless and free from the childish, anthropomorphic ideas about religion". Obviously, if one can harness the forces of chaos, one could be said to have supernatural powers. These could be the powers of Christ or of darker forces. It depends upon the intent of the user.

In summary of the last few chapters, we have traced the evolution of science to the point where it seeks to comprehend the predictability and consequent understanding of the entire universe. Where pure science ends, we are left with the void of creation. This includes the bizarre, the incredible and the fantastic. And while I have sought to enlighten everyone on the scientific logic of UFOs, the phenomena that comes with them cannot be termed to be other than bizarre.

It is with this in mind that we introduce the next part of this book which will include aliens, abductions, and implants. While these subjects are considered generally chaotic and crazy by the news media and some of the general population as well, it is important that these subjects be categorized with as much accuracy as possible. As a phenomenon, they can no longer be denied.

I will begin by discussing my own personal experiences which led to an encounter in the Pleiades.

11

Contact

    I grew up in a rather sickly fashion. There was a physical irregularity with my tongue, and I didn't talk until I was about five. As soon as this was discovered, my doctor performed an operation and I began to talk immediately. In fact, my mother said I was quite a chatterbox. I knew how to talk, but hadn't had the chance my entire life. Despite this improvement, I had frequent illnesses and problems. These climaxed at the age of twelve when I passed out twice as the result of a heart murmur.

    As I grew into my teens, things didn't get much better. I was far more uncoordinated at that age than the average teenager. We finally found out that I had some form of a neurological disease more popularly known as cerebral palsy. This means that while I was able to think and have an active mind, the signals were not getting to the muscular structure correctly and I consequently appeared to be very gawky.

    By the time I had reached seventeen, these problems had cleared up rather suddenly and without explanation. Although I could now physically do anything I wanted, my prior health history resulted in my family doctor arranging to have me declared 4-F with no examination by the military. It is possible I was already being slated as an employee for the Montauk Project.

While there is still no official explanation for my resurgence in health, it could possibly be connected to some very bizarre dreams I began to have at about the age of sixteen or seventeen. The most common dream was this big god who was blue eyed, blond haired and very human in appearance. He would take me with him and we would visit various places.

At about the same time that I began having these dreams, a voice suddenly appeared in my head. It was not demonic or negative but was very intelligent. I could carry on conversations with it.

Although my health had improved considerably, the dreams and the strange voice made me wonder what was going on. I had to consider whether I was crazy as these were obviously not "normal" experiences that society understood. As a result, I entered college and decided I would become a shrink. I subsequently learned that most psychology students pursue the subject in order to understand themselves. I definitely was in that category.

In the beginning, I was concerned that I might be suffering from multiple personality syndrome but that was soon dismissed. The knowledge I had obtained from my experiences was too broad based to be attributed to another identity lurking within my mental circuitry. There was something else going on of a higher order.

It was not long before I became the focus of my hypnosis class. I would be regressed and taken back to the times of my dreams. My hypnosis professor was convinced that I was sincere and that I thoroughly believed I had been taken into the confidence of tall blond "aliens" who were well built and stood seven to seven and a half feet in height.

Further regressions revealed that I believed these creatures to be very nice and benevolent. I had asked these aliens if they were going to hurt me and they said no. They responded that I must have been thinking of the Zetas (Grays) who do medical examinations that intrude into the body. I don't remember the name of this "god" but he told me his race didn't need to intrude physically. He had me stand by a pole from which he was able to do a complete read out on my medical condition. In total, I was regressed about eight times in front of the entire hypnosis class. This is somewhat remarkable because if someone tries to hypnotize me today, it doesn't work.

According to these regressions, I was taken into the confidence of the Pleiadians at about age fifteen and transported to their planet for medical rehabilitation and further education. Whether these encounters were in the dream state or in another constellation, I cannot really say. All I know is that after I had these experiences, I suddenly appeared to have a complete mastery of electronics. This was immediately noticeable to my parents and was most perplexing to them. I also had a guiding voice appear in my mind that would talk to me and tell me where to find answers to questions that I had. Whatever had occurred in the objective universe with these various experiences, my life had changed drastically for the better. I had gained incredible knowledge and a healthier body than I had previously experienced. The debilitating effects from the cerebral palsy even left.

It is important to keep these facts in mind when evaluating the relative truth of what the Pleiadians taught me about themselves and their planet.

12

The Pleiades

At about the age of fifteen, I was transported on a space ship to a small base located on one of the moons of Jupiter. I believe it was Europa. There, I was examined and put through a lot of testing. There were no bad memories from the experience. In fact, they were quite good. I even remember eating like a king. I was also shown their forms of entertainment which were very similar to ours. They included movies, video games and the like. It was apparent that these beings were essentially human and enjoyed the same things humans do.

I was then put on the ship again for a ride that lasted what I thought to be about an Earth day. I soon stepped into a very lush green and beautiful world they called Alderon. I was then taken through cities which had tall spires and buildings made of what appeared to be glass. The sky was blue and the visual scapes were breathtakingly beautiful. The air was quite crisp with no pollution. I was told the water was very pure. Long ago, there had been problems with pollution that had found its way into the food chain. This was corrected and they had gone back to the food chain long since.

The fauna and animal life on Alderon is very close in similarity to that of the Earth. The atmosphere is richer in oxygen than Earth's with a 28 to 30 percent content. The sunlight appears similar and the distance of their sun is more or less 93,000,000 miles away.

The primary difference between Earth and Alderon is the construction and landscaping. Where we have cities full of roads, macadam and homes, their planet is dominated by fauna and gardens. There are wide plains of grass and forests as well as large areas of primitive jungle. What I saw was an absolutely beautiful garden environment where the buildings were positioned in such a way as to accent the garden. The idea of this environment was that the ecosphere had priority. Oxygen replenishment was at the top of the list and human civilization was put in as an adjunct to the garden. It wasn't supposed to stand out but rather blend in with the garden environment.

I was given a tour of the city. The people looked just like humans and appeared very healthy. They did not appear to be controlled nor were they on drugs. From what I was told, the various individuals of the planet did what they were best suited for in accordance with what they wanted to do. There was no money system such as we know.

The buildings were a rectilinear type construction similar to our world except that the corners were rounded. There were no shingles or anything similar. The outside walls were a uniformed surface with the windows blended into the walls so that the smooth surface was maintained. Some of the buildings looked like they were of metallic construction while others appeared to be made of stone. There were different color schemes, but they were all designed to complement the landscape. Although none of the buildings were dome shaped or round, some of the structures had dome shaped windows which stood out like hemispherical bubbles.

The inside of the structures confused me and I couldn't figure out how the buildings were constructed. There were no panels or joints to reveal how things fit together. It looked like one amorphous wall. I could not see any welds on the walls, and I had to wonder if the whole configuration was molded in a big cast and put into place.

The interiors were very plain and usually consisted of a single color. Everything was very conservative with no stripes or cluttered patterns. The furniture was modern but also plain and appeared to be cast out of plastic. The furniture was similar to the buildings in that you couldn't see how it was constructed. They had reclining chairs with levers (but no screws). I tipped one over to look at it but couldn't understand the mechanisms.

The homes of the natives were typically single family units. Most of them were tastefully placed throughout the landscape. Aside from the rounded corners and plain surface, they were somewhat similar to suburban houses on Earth except that they blended in with the environment. The insides of the houses were again plainly furnished with solid colors. There was also art work which was absolutely beautiful. It consisted primarily of renditions of the planet's natural settings. One piece of art depicted a farm setting. They had some farms although much of their food was synthesized. There were also view screens which possessed a sound system, but I couldn't find any speakers. The audio might have been transmitted directly to the senses. I don't know.

There were no streets as we know them. Transport was by foot save for a public transporting device which would send you to any potential location. A port for this transportation service could be found in each home. There were no vehicles of any kind.

From the tour of the city, I was taken to what was called an education center. There, I was put through a process which they said gave me the equivalent of four different doctorate degrees on Earth. These were in the subjects of physics, electronics, psychology and divinity. They said this knowledge would eventually surface during my life on Earth.

While I was being educated, I was also taken to their medical center and put through a testing procedure. They got rid of the neurological problems I suffered from which would explain why the awkwardness in my own life disappeared practically overnight. They also got rid of the heart murmur.

My family doctor proclaimed this cure to be a miracle. He had checked my heart and heard a murmur loud and clear. One month later it was gone, but he didn't know why. Further neurological tests were done, but they found I had no more control problems. Obviously, I was very pleased with my new found friends in the Pleiades.

The Pleiadians are just people like you or I only they are more developed. They have been around much longer and they live longer. They live to about 1,000 of their years which equates to about 700 Earth years. Most of them looked almost as if they were carbon copies of each other. They all had blue eyes and blond hair, but their personalities were different. Their dress was plain and usually consisted of a single color. Health problems are virtually non existent.

While I received my education, I would go home in the evening with the Chief Scientist. The Pleiadians had hobby rooms and his was a lab in the back of his house. It ran along the entire length of the house and was probably 100 by 30 feet. It was very well equipped and incredibly neat. It consisted of super advanced electronics with only a few of the items having any recognizable controls. This was also the case with the electronic devices I saw in the government and science centers.

This man collected old technology in the same manner that I collect old radio equipment. It was his hobby and he enjoyed it. He told me that some of his collection went back thousands and thousands of years. Some of it even looked like equipment you could find on Earth today. Apparently, their research facilities had instruments like ours because this equipment is probably the most versatile for R&D (Research and Development). There is nothing that will replace a man working at a bench and trying out a circuit. I don't think there is any question that our civilization is based upon theirs. I even saw chairs that were very similar in operation to the Montauk Chair.

The Chief Scientist was my primary guide although there were others as well. They taught me about their star system and cultural inclinations.

Chapter Twelve — The Pleiades

There are six planets within the star cluster known as the Pleiades and they make up the society I will refer to as the Pleiades. Three of these worlds are very much like us in the physical world of development. Arian is the philosophical and religious center. Alderon is the technical center where science projects and manufacturing takes place. Aldebaran is the name of the planet that contains the center of defense. This is the group that fights their wars and is somewhat of a splinter group from the rest of the Pleiadian culture. They are very protective of their fellow Pleiadians; sometimes too much so.

The other three planets that make up Pleiadian society are not populated at all with human type beings. The beings on these planets are pure energy. On one of these three planets is the (non physical) high council. These are the twelve super beings that rule the Pleiadian culture. Each of the twelve have an equal say. They literally have the good of everybody at heart and might be identified in our culture as angels. None of the Pleiadian beings question the council or fight with them. It is unheard of.

You can understand this easier if you realize that I have yet to hear of a decision made by the council that was not a proper decision. I am talking about a harmonious free society that we would consider to be a utopia. The main reason they have achieved this evolved state is that they developed a collective consciousness which links them all together. This link manifests in the individual minds of the Pleiadians as a voice that can be conversed with. It is not a cacophony of voices nor does it give orders or seek to control a person. It is more like a companion or adviser. In this manner, each Pleiadian has a piece of the collective consciousness while retaining their own individuality. If mankind was linked in such a manner, I do not believe that there would be any war or crime on Earth. We actually already have this faculty but it is a subconscious link which we are not aware of on a conscious level. I know it is there because I have personally developed a link to the human Earth consciousness, but I do not hear a voice as I do in the case of the Pleiadian consciousness. If we fully develop this faculty, it would probably appear as a voice.

The Pleiadian voice usually just gives me advice or tells me where to find answers to different questions. At times, I can become very exasperated with the voice because it won't answer direct questions but only tells me where to find answers.

According to what I learned, the history of the Pleiadian civilization goes back into antiquity. It is over 100,000 Earth years old and originates from what they refer to as the Old Universe. They came through a barrier and entered this part of our galaxy. They settled amongst the seven sister stars which we call the Pleiades on our star maps. They are quite positive that they were a settlement that did not originate in this galaxy.

Their definition of the Old Universe is somewhat vague. It is something like the universe that the Creator originally created and loosely parallels the Star Wars saga by George Lucas. The Old Universe was very much like this one. There were problems with it so we created our own universe (this physical universe) and came through barriers as we entered. None of this is really too clear and recollections of it are like a genetic memory. Many people pick up on the Old Universe in their dreams.

The Pleiadians said they believed in a Creator. Any being with a piece of the Creator (we would call this "piece" the soul) is a son of the Creator. They said that Christ was a projection from the collective subconscious of our planet. This is the aspect of us that connects us to the Creator. Christ appeared on Earth in the spirit of "kicking us in the butt" to get us going with the Creator again.

I do not know the entire agenda of the Pleiadians. From what I can figure out, it seems to be twofold. First, they want to help us here on Earth because they believe a very key step in the evolution of this galaxy starts on this planet. They also like to see things take a natural course because they are super naturalists. Their other agenda is anthropological in that their interest is motivated by their belief that we are experiencing today what they went through hundreds of thousands of years ago. Their civilization started out much like ours and they are gaining insights by studying us and other similar groups in the galaxy.

The Pleiadian philosophy is very simple. They act with a "noninterference directive" with everybody and anybody, including themselves. They are designed to be a totally free society. What I mean here is that each individual is encouraged to pick up a mission or job. As long as that job fits in and is productive for the society, the individual is provided for.

In the Pleiades, there is no crime as we know it. Being part of a collective consciousness, any crime perpetrated would be against themselves. As long as they are part of the collective and subscribe to the philosophies of the collective, they don't have any crime per se. The only real crime a Pleiadian can commit, and certainly the biggest one, is to interfere with another person or civilization. I cannot stress how much they believe in this principle. If there is an interference, the penalty is death. The Pleiadians believe this to be not only a physical death but a spiritual one too. They are very strict on this point.

The above reasoning is why the Pleiadians stock planets with representatives by utilizing the natives on the planet concerned. They make contacts and communicate with the various beings. If these beings agree with the Pleiadian philosophy, they will act as ambassadors. I believe that I am one of these ambassadors, and I am quick to add that there are thousands of us. We are virtually unknown but are injecting the planet with an unknown (to most sources) but very peaceful influence. This is why we don't condone any sort of violence or terrorist acts. We don't even condone any civil disobedience. Of course, it must be remembered that we are humans as well as Pleiadians and therefore can't be held one hundred percent accountable to this ideal.

I must point out that while I believe I am an ambassador for the Pleiadians and their agenda seems to be peace and love, I do not have a complete knowledge of the entire circumstances. My Pleiadian contacts have not given me any cause to disbelieve them, but it is not necessarily my prerogative to give them a full endorsement without critical analysis.

For example, they believe they were the ones who originally colonized this planet but others will debate that it was done first by Marduk or Orion. I think these various groups all established colonies here at about the same general time period.

Others will also be suspicious of the Pleiadians because of their supposed involvement with Hitler and the Third Reich. This is standard fodder in UFOlogy so should be commented on. According to my contacts, Hitler was told to preserve the Aryan (same as Pleiadian) seed here on Earth. He was not supposed to kill off the seed of the Pleiadians arch enemies, the Draco, who colonized Earth in the form of the Semitic race. His mission was to protect the Aryans from the Semites and make an Aryan country for those who wanted to come and live in an exclusive Aryan environment. Of course, a lot of concepts and signals got crossed. Hitler did not pursue his mission and went off the rails, to say the least.

As I said earlier, the agenda of the Pleiadians seems to be peace and love. I believe this also includes the process of education. We have to retain our own discernment and not fall into the belief systems that mind control organizations try to foster upon civilization. I must therefore embrace my own Pleiadian contacts as bizarre but positive phenomena which cannot be denied or ignored.

I have seriously examined this phenomena since I was twenty-five and sought out objective points of view. The most convincing corroboration that these contacts were real came in about 1991.

One day, I received a call from somebody who told me to go to the Gardiner Manor Shopping Mall at four o'clock in the afternoon. I made the trip to the mall, walked in and everything was fine. The lights were on and a number of people were in the shopping mall. As I stepped from the entrance corridor to the main corridor, it was as if I had walked through a wall. Suddenly, the mall became dark. The lights were off and there was virtually no one in the mall. I felt as if time had "jumped". I walked around and tried to figure out what was going on. I soon found a guard and exchanged greetings with him. The clock indicated it was three in the morning.

I then saw a lighted corridor that went in the opposite direction from the entrance. I now remembered that I had been directed to go down this corridor in the original phone call I had received. Going down that corridor I found three men who were supposed to be Pleiadian contacts. Afterwards, I wrote a message on a piece of paper for my own benefit that read "I was here at 3:00 a.m.". I then stashed it in a potted plant in hopes of retrieving it later and verifying my experience. The memories are somewhat hazy, but I ended up having Pleiadian contacts or dreams that evening.

Upon waking the next morning, I recalled some of the experiences and decided I would return to the mall and try and find the note I'd left in the potted plant. Upon entering the mall, I noticed the same security guard and spoke to him. He remembered me and relayed that he should have challenged me for being at the mall after closing hours, but for some reason he didn't bother me. Something had apparently affected his mood or behavior. It wasn't long before I got to the potted plant and found the note I had left for myself. All of this verified to me beyond the shadow of a doubt that some contacts of a paranormal sort had taken place. It wasn't an hallucination. As far as I am concerned and based upon the experiences I have relayed to you in this book, the contacts I have had with the Pleiadians are real.

13

Aliens

Although my contacts to the aliens are through the Pleiadians, it does not mean that we should advocate their consciousness only. There are plenty of other creatures on the scene and in the interest of education, I will inform you what I know of the different alien races involved in our planet. My information is based upon my contacts with the Pleiadians, my own personal experiences plus what I have absorbed from my contacts in the defense industry.

There are all types of alien life beginning with the lower order life forms on other planets. Obviously, a low order form of life will not build a space ship or even a car. In order to build something, a life form has to be able to conceptualize. This takes a being of a very high order.

In discussing aliens, I am not going to consider the lower order life forms on other planets. The aliens we are interested in are the ones that can accomplish space travel in order to visit the Earth and elsewhere. Assembling a space ship requires a being of a very high order with a complex dynamic function (sometimes called the quantum dynamic function) which is commonly called the soul. In common terms, a soul is a being with enough of a dynamic function burned into the space time continuum to have a consciousness. This means that you yourself are a quantum dynamic function and are partially composed of chaos or, if you prefer, random probability and unpredictability. In computer terms, a soul refers to a self sustaining software program that can receive, send, process and originate information. We can therefore rule out the lower order of plants, animals, and insects which primarily respond only to instinct or programming. The aliens we will be looking at will have to have a consciousness and soul or soul like consciousness that can reason, deduct and generate its own programming.

There are a number of different types of aliens, but the most common form derives from the mammalian or animal world. These are human beings or human like beings that are based upon the animal life from different planets. These types of aliens will come from a world somewhat similar to Earth in that it will require the same type of fauna and environment required to support animal life. The animals from one planet to another will have common similarities although there will be differences as well. A dog on another planet may look a little different, but it will most likely have the same biological status that a dog on Earth has. Besides mammals, you will also find microbes, plant, insect, and reptilian life that are all carbon based (as is all life on Earth). The reason that Earth type planets (which contain life that is carbon based) are the most common is that carbon, oxygen and hydrogen interact with each other more easily than do other elements. To go into ammonia and nitrogen requires a more difficult molecular structure that is not as conducive to evolution. It is for this reason that most life, including alien life, is carbon or hydrocarbon based. The geometry of the molecules makes a better fit.

All of this means that the most common forms of alien life will be animal like human beings. Pleiadians are animal or human based. Their genetic code is similar to that of monkeys. The K Group or Krundeshen,* as I believe they are called, are also human based. In fact, they are so human that they are bald. If you put a hair piece on one, they can pass for a human. While they are similar in height to us,

---
* The name Krundeshen was channeled by Duncan Cameron.

the Pleiadians are much taller. There are many more groups within our galaxy which are human like. This can include life forms such as cat people, dog people or bear people. These would all fall into the category of mammalian because their genetic base is not that far off from that of a human or simian form.

In addition to the mammalians, you will have reptilian like beings as well as insectoids. Most of these life forms appear to be bipedal and humanoid. Some of them may have extra arms or legs, but two legs and two arms with a torso seems to be the most common and efficient form of life. It mostly has to do with the practical factors of evolution. There are, of course, various mutations and variations that will pop up from time to time.

The most common type of reptilian looks like a cross between an alligator and human. One can get an idea of what this type of reptilian looks like by viewing an old *Star Trek* show where a creature called a Gorn fought Captain Kirk at the insistence of a group of other beings called Metrons. Revealing themselves at the end of the episode, the Metrons looked very much like the Pleiadians I have described except that they were shorter. Hollywood has always had an uncanny ability to tap into the collective subconscious of man and this is apparently just one more example. Reptilians such as the Gorn are relatively common in our galaxy although not all of them have such a big snout. Reptilians are typically slow but very strong and usually at odds with the humans and/or Pleiadians. They have tremendous psychic abilities and can hypnotize people simply by looking at them.

After mammalians and reptilians, the most common form of alien life are the insectoids. The most often encountered form of insectoids are the grays which are actually a cross breeding of insects with the reptilians. The grays have the traits of reptilians in their eyes but their skeletons frame the outside of their body (referred to as exoskeletons). Reptilians and mammalians have an inner skeleton. There is a famous video tape that shows what appears to be a sort of gray like being dying. The creature is literally thrashing around in an extremely fast manner. Isolating the video frames, one can see that the thing is turning within 1/30th of a second. Neither reptilians nor mammals move that fast but most insect creatures can. The grays also have the hypnotic powers of the reptilians but often serve in subjugation to them.

The grays are not the only insectoid race, but they are the most popular in current UFOlogy. There is also an alien that looks very much like a six to seven foot tall praying mantis. These aliens are very loving and foster healing. They are not warlike at all.

Other types of aliens include winged humanoids or bird people. These really come under the heading of reptilian because birds are zoologically considered to be reptilians although they are warm blooded. Most intelligent reptilian life forms are warm blooded because the cold blooded reptilians are not as advanced. There is also a fourth class of alien life that has been theorized. This is an intelligent plant with a cellulose base. I have never heard any reports of this type of life form, but it remains a possibility.

There are also the nonphysical beings of pure intelligence which I referred to in my discussion of the Pleiadians. They also act as high council and promote the group consciousness that extends throughout the Pleiadian culture. The reptilians and other advanced life forms likewise have a group consciousness. This faculty seems to be a stage of evolutionary development which ties all the "bio-netware" of a particular race together.

Those mentioned above are not the only aliens in the universe, but they are the ones I am familiar with and are also the basic types of life in the galaxy. Next, we will look at how they have colonized Earth.

14

Colonization

From what I've been told, the Pleiadians did the first genetic engineering of apes into human beings and established the original settlement on Earth. Humans are so close genetically to Pleiadians that they can cross breed with them without any problems. In fact, we are so close to the Pleiadians that all humans today are probably derived from them. Other races of beings have also stepped in and have genetically engineered the original seed of man to be closer to their own genetic structure.

The Caucasian or Aryan races would be the original race fostered by the Pleiadian consciousness. The oriental race is rumored to be a genetic alteration of the Pleiadians by the grays (insectoid). This could explain why orientals have slanted eyes and have a worker bee mentality. All of this information is supposition based upon suggestions and informed sources. It should not offend anyone and is not meant to do so.

The next race to appear were the Abernache. They came from the planet Marduk as cited by Sitchin in *The Twelfth Planet*. They were supposedly a white race that genetically engineered the black race. The purest black race on Earth were known as the Nubians and are considered to be natives of this planet. Their genetic structure was crossed with the Pleiadians to give us the black race that we know today. Marduk was also known as Nemesis or Bκte Noir in French, meaning "black beast".

The Reptilians from Orion took the Pleiadian seed race and modified it to create the Semitic race. This explains why the Aryan race is sometimes called the master race. The theory is that it was the original blueprint which was doctored to fit the agenda of a particular life form.

In addition to the above races, there is also the Native American race. Although most of their legends indicate they come from the Pleiades, this is not actually correct. Their identification with the Pleiades comes from the cultural influence of Atlantis which was a Pleiadian settlement and the most recent ruling power in their history. The Native Americans are believed to have derived from a being that looked very human but was red haired and red bearded and came from the Andromedan galaxy.

If you take the above four races and interbreed them, you will have the brown race which can be considered a mixture of caucasians, blacks and orientals or some combination thereof. There are other possibilities as well.

Please understand that I am not saying that any one race is more or less intelligent than the others. I am just trying to demonstrate how different alien beings have intervened with mankind to produce the different races of man and the cultural melting pot we have on Earth.

The *Keys of Enoch* by J.J. Hurtak indicates that our planet ties its roots to the Elohim which traces back to the Orion and Pleiadian constellations. I believe this is correct because most of the interference in our history has come out of that sector.

This gives a general outline of how the Earth has been colonized. We will now look at some of the motivations and orientations of the different alien groups.

15
Alien Confederations

In our galaxy, we have three groups or confederations. The terms used to describe them were originally channeled by Duncan Cameron from his information source. These are the Neverons, the Galactic Confederation, and the Leverons.

The Neveron group is really just a name for the Pleiadian Confederation which we have already discussed. Sometimes considered to be "the good guys", they have a strict noninterference directive.

The Galactic Confederation parallels the United Nations we have on this planet. It consists of many different groups that got together and formed a confederation of planets. They are pretty much neutral and also have a noninterference directive which is derived from the Pleiadian Confederation or Neverons but is not as severe. While the Galactic Confederation has a code which allows them to interfere to maintain balance or save one of their own, the Pleiadian noninterference code is absolutely unconditional. Even if the Pleiadians lose a battle cruiser on this planet, they are forbidden from blowing a city away in order to retrieve their cruiser. They would most likely send operatives to destroy the craft and keep it out of other hands.

"The third group is the Leverons. Duncan actually channeled a long and complicated spelling, but I use the simple phonetic spelling "Leveron". The word "leviathan" (which can be etymologically traced to the word "snake") derived from this group called the Leverons. They represent the archetype of a devil or super negative being. This is the negative side. They will step on people in order to get what they want and enforce the idea that the end justifies the means. The Leveron alliance consists of reptilians and grays and their leader is from a planet called Draco which orbits Draco Major in the Orion constellation. That is why the Leverons are sometimes referred to as the Orion alliance.

There is also a group of Pleiadians who tie into the Orion alliance. They are rebels and fighters, but they are fiercely protective of their other fellow Pleiadians. There are actually three groups of Pleiadians. First are the Arian Pleiadians which is where the term "Aryan" came from. They are philosophers, thinkers and dreamers. Some of them will not fight under any circumstances. The Alderon Pleiadians are doers. They also think well but are oriented towards doing things. This name is also used in the Star Wars movie. They are sort of in between the Arian philosophers and soldiers which comprise the third group: the Aldebaran Pleiadians. These are commonly called the negative Pleiadians. They are the ones who contacted Hitler and sent him off to protect and foster the Aryan race. They thought they were protecting their brothers and have been known to take their concerns to extremes. Although the Aldebarans are Pleiadians, they align more with the Orion group. They do not religiously follow the noninterference code of the other Pleiadians and might come to this planet to rescue a Pleiadian from one of the other two groups.

I don't know how the Draconians are set up, but there are at least three different versions of them. Some of the Draconian alliance even appear to be quite human. They are not all reptilian or insectoid in appearance.

With the different agendas that have been referred to, it is obvious that there is conflict in the universe. There is the Pleiadian Alliance which wants no interference of any kind. Then, there is the Galactic Confederation which wants conditional interference. Finally, there is the Leverons or Orions who require major interference and want to run the entire show and annex Earth to the Draconian Empire. All of this results in the basic strife we see here: the battle for planet Earth. This weaves its way most subtly into the entire cultural fabric of society. It includes the air we breath, the food we eat, the vehicles we drive, the money we use, the shows we watch, the music we listen to, the politicians we vote for and just about everything else.

In simple terms, life on Earth is not left to itself and allowed to evolve on its own terms. There is interference and meddling. One group is seeking control over another and some will not stop at the prospect of using forceful means to accomplish their ends. This brings us to the most sinister way to subjugate the population of Earth: abduction and implants."

16
Abductions

Most abductions can be classified into one of two groups: alien or government. First, I should clarify that when I say "government", I am not referring to our duly elected officials but a secretive and mysterious "Illuminati" sort of group that functions through all arms of society. Through their own means of conscious and malicious controls over the minds of others, this group infiltrates all levels of the culture but concentrates on power points such as the military, major corporations, and all spheres of influence including the government.

It is interesting to point out that quite a few television programs in the mid 1990s have reported on the alien abduction phenomena. It gives one the impression that "the truth" is coming to the surface. There is a good reason that alien abductions have been given so much air play. The government does their own abductions and wants you to believe it is all coming from outer space. This sort of charade goes even deeper. Many people who begin to recall the surface memories of actual government abductions instead think they are recalling an alien encounter. A surface memory has been placed over the deeper memory so you'll think you were abducted by aliens instead of the government. It is most convenient for the government to blame all abductions on aliens.

According to some estimates, the government is accountable for most abductions with the grays being responsible for approximately twenty to thirty percent.

Under the category of aliens, we have three classes of abductions: physical, astral and induction. Physical abductions refer to literally taking someone physically, putting them on a table and doing whatever is to be done with them. Astral abductions refer to taking the being or astral soul out of the body and manipulating such by electronic or more subtle means. Induction is when someone astrally enters the realm of another being and goes to work. If this type of manipulation is done on you, it might be something you are not even aware of.

Many abductees report being literally pulled through the walls of their house. This is usually a physical abduction because the aliens have technology capable of making you weightless and massless so that you can be pulled through a wall. This can also be an astral phenomena, but my research indicates it is usually physical.

Physical abductions usually include the removing of sexual samples. In females, they will usually take out an ovum or egg. In males, they will remove sperm cells. Aliens have also been known to take a biopsy of a testicle in the male or the ovaries in the female. In this case, they cut the skin behind the scrotum and remove the testicles by pulling them out of the sack. There is actually enough tube so that it can be shown to the patient. After hearing this report, I checked with a medical doctor who informed me there is about forty feet of tube within the scrotum.* The sperm cells are actually stored in the tube between the testicles and the prostate gland. Although these reports are primarily based on regressions, there is nothing biologically impossible about the descriptions. In all of these cases, the aliens are definitely taking procreative genetic samplings.

There are also operations where samples are taken from the stomach lining of either the male or the female. A big needle is inserted in the navel and a biopsy

---

* This sort of operation could perhaps explain the phenomena I spoke of earlier with regard to von Neumann having an extremely large scrotum.

is taken. If one can obtain what are called the stem cells or primary cells, then one can actually clone the body. These stem cells carry the whole DNA in its primary form. Geneticists are beginning to realize that as primary cells differentiate and replicate into secondary cells, the DNA changes. These primary or stem cells are most commonly found in the stomach, mouth, anal area and other portions of the body which interface with the outside world. The gonadal cells such as the testes or ovaries are also primary cells. They carry the entire genetic code of the organism. All of this suggests that the physical abductions done by the aliens are some sort of genetic research.

As so many abductees report having been shown offspring that were half alien and half human, there is really no question someone is attempting to cross breed the alien genetics with human genetics. One possible reason for this is that the alien race is very old and dying. Over time, their genetics have either "atrophied" or become distorted to the point where they are now trying to regain the youthful genetics of our race. It is as if they are doing damage control by combining our genes with theirs. All of this suggests that any aliens engaging in such activity have a similar genetic base to ours.

Many female abductees remember copulating with a male space person or alien. In these cases, the aliens let the fetus grow for two months (some people say three) whereupon the female is abducted again with the fetus being removed. In these cases, the woman discovers that she is pregnant but has no idea how she became so. Two months later, the pregnancy disappears. These reports are very common from female abductees around the country.

There are at least two possibilities that could have happened in these cases. One is actual fertilization by the alien male as mentioned above. The other alternative possibility is that the initial sampling of the woman is fertilized in a test tube with alien DNA and then placed into the woman's womb for a couple of months. The woman is then abducted again, the fetus being removed as it is now old enough to incubate. It then grows into whatever it is going to be. This latter possibility is corroborated by reports that describe beings that are partially human and partially another life form such as plant like, reptilian or whatever.

Genetic sampling and breeding is not the only purpose of physical abductions. Aliens also do implantation. Sometimes it is a simple matter of putting in a transponder which is in reality a transceiver (a device which both transmits and receives). This receiver is tuned to a certain frequency and is keyed to recognize a certain code. When that code is received by the transponder, it triggers a transmission which enables the aliens to locate you so that they can abduct you again. They have to have a system. If they are taking a woman, implanting her with a fetus and then removing the fetus two months later, they have to be able to find that woman when they want. If they are taking genetic samples from men, they have to do the same.

In the case of male abductions, semen samples are taken with regularity and not just once. One abductee who underwent therapy to have his abductions stopped was successful in that regard but ended up with a disease caused by excess sperm cells. He was so used to having his seminal tube between the testicles and prostate being cleared out by the aliens that he had never masturbated. This build up causes the sperm cells to rot after a while and he began to get infections in the scrotum. This was diagnosed by a doctor who taught him to clear his tubes from time to time.

Most of the physical abductions are genetic examinations or implantations of some sort. This includes conditioning and programming as well. The implants themselves are usually surgically inserted in the body. They are not simply shot in with a syringe or cruder means. Scars can be found but they are very very thin and are disguised so that you won't find them unless you know what you are looking for. Age lines can masquerade as implant scars. More obvious ones are scoop marks found on the arms, legs or anywhere else on the body. Sometimes a thin thread like mark will be found along the spine or near the sexual organs.

Chapter Sixteen — Abductions

Most of the physical abductions are performed by the gray aliens or "government". The government performs all sorts of clandestine medical research through their abductions and then blames it on the aliens. I'm not saying the aliens are good or bad, but it is obvious we are looking at two different agendas when it comes to this subject. The prospect of alien agendas, as we have already discussed, are quite disturbing but the government's agenda sounds even more frightening.

While the government does take some blood samples and what not, genetic research has not traditionally been their main area of study. They are primarily into medical research which includes conditioning, implanting and physical implants (silicon chip sets).

If you hypnotize a typical abductee, you will soon come to the aliens. This is surface memory. If you take the abductee deeper into the subconscious by using other routines, all of a sudden the aliens will become human beings. They will usually be attired in a recognizable military uniform. There is no conceivable reason that the aliens would implant a memory so deep into the subconscious. If they wanted us to think their abductions were conducted by the military, they would put the false memory of the human abductions in the upper subconscious and not the lower subconscious.

There are two levels of technology used for physical abductions. Many times, the aliens will literally take a human out of their car. We know that the person was actually taken out of the car because upon their return, they find themselves in another location and have to retrieve their car. In these cases, a technology is employed where the human is teleported to and from the space ship. As they reach or leave a particular destination, they may float along in space before coming to a full stop. The second technology is the government just coming and grabbing or kidnapping someone. If anyone else is in the house, they will be put into an unconscious state. Aliens will also put out people that they don't want, but these instances usually turn out to be government abductions.

There are many programs administered under the heading of "government abductions". One of the major programs is the abduction of children to program them and then have them develop into a sort of super secret army force that will activate in the event of national chaos. They are programmed to carry out the agenda of the powers that be which will fluctuate from time to time but will ultimately be concerned with control.

This physical programming by the government is administered with an electroshock system that is very similar to the electroshock machine used in insane asylums. A particularly effective technique they employ will literally electrically stimulate the person to the height of sexuality. Once the subject is excited to the highest point (just before ejaculation in the male and just before the contraction of the vaginal walls in the female), they suspend the state so the person's consciousness and physicality is suspended in an orgasmic state. The mind is in suspension and is technically quite wide open. At that point, all they have to do is pick up a block of memory and put it in. The technology has been developed to where almost any agent can do it. The electroshocking of the person is computer run and the program is put on a floppy disk which can then be placed into a portable computer. With this advance in technology, the only other thing an agent needs is a diagram to wire the subject up.

The agent first subdues the victim in one fashion or another. He then wires him or her up, boots up the computer, puts in the floppy disk and runs the program. The method of moving one block of memory to another and hiding memories is all canned. They also implant thoughts into different sections of the mind. Each time the subject goes into a sexual state, the thought is being programmed through the whole being. Such people are usually programmed to have sex so as to keep the implant active.

People who have been sexually programmed in the above manner also transmit whatever information was programmed into them whenever they go into a sexual state. Sexual ecstasy is a rather magnetic and hypnotic state and it is said to contain "magic". In such a state, one partner can transmit to the other according to what was programmed. One can even be subconsciously indoctrinated to control their copulation to the point where they can transmit to the partner without either party being aware of what is going on. A "mind meld" occurs. Some young men are programmed to such a degree that they can miraculously arouse tremendous desire in a woman. If the programmers want a program spread around, such young men sow their seed around with the programming of the women concerned being the target. In this manner, an idea or program can be inserted into the society on a wholesale basis. It could be as simple a program as "buy ABC detergent", vote for this politician or it could be considerably more complex. In some of these men, the magnetism is working overtime to where they can copulate two or three times a day, sometimes with more than one woman. These men are like incubuses and can have quite a devastating even if romantic effect on females. My estimate is that about ten percent of the male population under thirty have been programmed in this manner.

Conditioning is related to programming, but it is a different procedure. The most common kind of conditioning also uses electroshock. Two electrodes are placed on the sides of the subject's forehead and a picture is placed in front of him or her. The picture is designed to influence the person. Let's say they want to train people to hate the President. They will put the President's face on a screen and shock the subject. After a while, the person is going to react every time he see a picture of the President or has him brought to mind. He will go into a panic and will learn to hate the President.

Conditioning is also used to control a person's behavior. Let's say there is a particular response they don't want someone to have. They will take the subject and do something to trigger that response and then shock them at that exact point. Over time, the person will subconsciously do anything possible to avoid that response. Different and more complex circumstances can easily be conceived, but these are the basic principles of conditioning.

The aliens don't have any need for conditioning. In fact, I have never heard of a true alien abduction where electroshock was used. They are not that crude. If they want to influence someone's mind, they have more sophisticated techniques such as astral programming.

Astral programming is when they remove the spirit, astral being or whatever you want to call it. We are talking about the essence of you that is not physical. All of us leave our body at night and astral travel. Some of us are more aware of it than others. Becoming aware in your dreams and actually assuming consciousness in that state is an ancient occult technique and is today popularly referred to as lucid dreaming. True astral travel is when you can leave your body, travel out to the environment and view objective situations and people. Some people can actually get solid enough in the astral plane to where they can appear in physical form. This principle is sometimes used to explain the resurrection of Christ. If one has fully developed this faculty, one can actually bilocate and accomplish tasks in another place.

Just as aliens have the capability of taking us away physically, they can also take us out of our body and back to their ship. Astral abductions are actually energetic abductions. Aliens sometimes just want to sample our energy. They might want to sample our patterns or get a read out of our energy body since the last time we were abducted. They also might want to program us so that we will do and say what they want. Astral programming does work and is done all the time. It was and is used quite frequently at Montauk.

Astral abductions can be mistaken for the physical abductions because there isn't much difference. Either the astral being is floating out of the body or the body has become weightless and is floating along with the aliens. If you want to know if something was done physically to your body, you can look for scoop marks. Pain is not a good measure because pain can be inflicted astrally.

As the government is quite capable of doing physical abductions, they are also capable of working on the astral but it is not the usual method of operation. They have a Psi

Chapter Sixteen — Abductions

Corps which can pull a person out of the body and have a psychic operator mind meld with an abductee and drain the mind of memories. As with the aliens, read outs are done from the last abduction. This is how spies can be read out without even being aware they are spies. At night, a spy is abducted by the Psi Corp. The mind meld is done and what the spy saw is known and recorded. If they want, they can also abduct the subject physically and do whatever they want. I will later discuss a class of implants that do the same thing, but implants are not capable of interrogating the memory. They can only transmit what our senses are picking up.

There are also cases where the aliens and government work together. This is based upon the idea that we have some sort of treaty with the grays from Rigel. The government hides behind this umbrella at every opportunity.

Besides physical and astral abductions, there is also the third class I referred to earlier as induction. This is where they go into your nonphysical being and do their readouts and programming. This is different from the astral abductions in that they are coming into you instead of taking you away. I think this is done by a different alien group and one that is more advanced that the grays. These aliens (probably the reptilians) are able to leave their body just as you are. They are not physical when they enter you and are advanced enough to know how to get into the being during a vulnerable state, cohabit the body with the host and do whatever their work is. The induction can last for seconds, hours or months and appears to be used for the same ends as the physical and astral abductions. To my knowledge, the government has not been successful with this technique.

As some people might confuse induction with a "walk in", I want to clarify that phenomenon. A "walk in" refers to a spirit coming into a body previously occupied by someone else. It usually happens after a trauma to the original host. Let's say someone was frightened to death and left the body over sheer fear. If the body is still operable, another being comes in and animates it even though it might have been clinically dead for a short while. This is known as a "walk in". Of course, the walk in could have been generated by the spirit walking in. He could have frightened the original host because he wanted the body.

A "walk in" may occur in many other instances. Let's say Uncle Hector sexually molested Johnny when he was seven years old. Johnny found it so terrible that he decided to leave instead of experiencing the molestation. Next thing you know, Johnny is gone. Before Uncle Hector realizes that the body is dead, another being steps in and takes over. The parents then notice tremendous changes in the child. Later on, the parents might find out that Uncle Hector was molesting the child and they chalk up the drastic change to be a result of the abuse. They never considered that Johnny is no longer Johnny but is now Billy. He rapidly learns to respond to the name Johnny and the life that goes with it.

A "shove in" or a "force in" is yet a different phenomenon. This is where someone forcefully pulls a being out of a body and shoves in another spirit.

While there are many elaborate scenarios that can be envisioned, these are the basics of alien and government implants to the best of my knowledge. I have also written more about this subject in my other books concerning the Montauk Project.

17
Have You Been Abducted?

After reading the previous chapter, I imagine the next thing you as the reader will be interested in is whether or not you have been abducted and if so, what can be done about it.

Many people who have been abducted are already quite certain of it. Others have had subjective experiences they are not sure of or simply want confirmation of what they feel did happen to them. Many want to know how to tell whether or not they were abducted.

Recognition of an abduction or alien interface will usually occur first in your dreams. It is typical for memory blocks that were implanted in your memory to erode with consequent leaks of implanted memories surfacing in the dream state. After this, the next level is actually remembering your abduction memories. You will swear that you were taken aboard a UFO and worked upon. If you follow this memory even further, you might yet discover that the alien memory was actually a cover for a human abduction that might have occurred in the back of a meat truck or the like.

Further indications of being abducted also include the following: memory loss, missing time, a pronounced and continued ringing in the ears, waking up inexplicably in the middle of the night, and sudden psychic abilities appearing that are not otherwise explained.

Many people will have further inquiries and may want to seek out somebody so they can be regressed to the time period in question. There are different techniques and you will want to find something that is comfortable for you. Deprogramming is too heavy a word for what I am referring to here. Usually, one is taken by hypnosis through different layers of consciousness. Unfortunately, ordinary hypnosis generally only penetrates the first two layers of consciousness and the real information is often missed. The aliens and the government seek to bury their dirty work which is usually found in the third or fourth layers of consciousness. There is also a fifth level of consciousness which the government and aliens have trouble reaching. This is the area where the physical mind reaches the nonphysical mind.

I know people will ask me to elaborate on these different levels of consciousness, so I will be quick to say that I am being somewhat bold in defining them. These are rather arbitrary divisions based upon the average responses of people I have observed. If you work with people in this type of work, you will eventually recognize these layers of consciousness on your own although you might want to give them different names. There are many levels of physical consciousness which have never really been scientifically categorized in text books. Accurate information about the human mind is deliberately confused. Some books say there are four nonphysical levels of consciousness, but I believe there are more. This area is the most difficult to penetrate because beings are usually wrapped in the more physical aspects.

This last aspect is your saving grace as regards true abductions. In other words, there are aspects of the spirit which no one can penetrate, not even the most subtle and ingenious of aliens. The best line of defense to abductions is to just say "no". It is an esoteric truth that nothing can effect you unless you yourself allow it or give permission for it to occur. Of course, saying "no" may not be so easy. In that case, you will want to find someone you trust that can work with you. But, you should never lose sight of the fact that you ultimately have the direct ability to determine your own fate.

There is also a higher level phenomenon of "abduction" where the subject concerned feels he is communicating with aliens within the confines of his own conscious will. He or she may be going to different dimensions and exploring various aspects of existence with no trauma being present. Even so, these people sometimes need help with the various things they encounter.

For those who have serious problems or are dealing with such subjects, it should be realized that one's sexuality must be cleared out first. The reason for this is that this is the deep level where people's programming resides. If this area is cleared up, all the other blocks will clear out fast. But, one must be very careful. A wise practitioner will only allow a bit of trauma to surface at a time. Too much could be overwhelming to the subject. We all possess trauma. You may not feel anything now, but you likely have sustained injuries during your life that were accompanied by pain and emotional trauma. It may not be in your mind now, but it is stored away in a place where you don't remember it anymore. If you start downloading your mind, you will feel the pain once again.

The government will hide their programming behind the trauma in your mind. They also set it up so that if you go into the region of your mind where your ESP (extra sensory perception) is stored, you will find trauma. This lowers your psychic ability. The more trauma you have, the less ESP will be present because your third and fourth level of subconscious is occupied with the trauma. Consequently, almost anyone can multiply their ESP powers simply by clearing out the level of the mind where the ESP comes from.

When either the aliens or the government bury memories of an abduction below the trauma, they have done a very ingenious thing. As soon as you approach the area, you're going to panic because you can see all your trauma. I have witnessed people who tried to undergo fast deprogramming which unfortunately resulted in all their traumas surfacing at once. Two of these people were cocky and thought they could handle it. Both flipped out and one even had a car crash. Both practitioners and abductees should keep these factors in mind when they penetrate the deeper layers of consciousness.

18
Implants

Just as we spoke about physical and astral abductions, there are also physical and astral implants. In the course of my work, I've actually seen a unit of thought placed into the auric field encompassing a person's body. This is a typical astral implant which acts as a unit by itself in sending out its influences or readings.

Physical implants break down into two categories: inert implants and biological implants. An inert or purely physical implant is a piece of metal, crystal, silicon chip or other substance which is inserted into the body. These are designed to transmit right into the subject's nervous system. I recently found out that many of these implants are biological. When a subject for biological implanting is picked up, a sample of their cell structure is taken. The abductors then do some genetic engineering on the DNA and cell structure, culture it and grow a transceiver out of the biological matter. This sounds more than a bit avant garde, but there is no scientific research which indicates that a biological material cannot be configured to manufacture a radio transceiver. Where a normal transceiver would have wires, a biological version uses bionic cell structures that replicate the wire and other circuitry.

One implant has been discovered that is typically inserted in the body just above the gonads in the male. I'm not sure exactly where it would sit in the female. The implant is designed to transmit when the subject becomes sexually excited. If the subject is not excited then no transmission will occur.

Although these implants are often connected to sexuality, it is not always the case. I found one instance where this type of implant was also connected to the optical center of the brain. In other words, as I waved my hand in front of one guy's eyes and face, the transmission of the implant changed.

A bizarre and graphic example of a biological implant came to light when a fellow from Brooklyn visited me and wanted to be scanned for implants. At that particular time, I was using spectrum analyzers, grid dip oscillators (this is a device which looks for resonant networks) and other equipment in order to find implants with radio circuitry in them. As I moved an RF (radio frequency) probe over his body, I noticed a signal appeared when I brought it close to his abdomen. If I took the probe away from his abdomen, the signal went down and almost disappeared on the spectrum analyzer. Of course, anyone who works with electronics knows spectrum analyzers aren't that accurate, so I had to "zero beat" the signal. This means that I put the signal into an analyzer so that it could be matched up with the signal being transmitted through this guy's body and identified. I wanted to find out the actual carrier frequency that the implant was on and I did. Lo and behold: it was the same as Channel 25 in Brooklyn!

This was a rather amazing discovery and was rather unbelievable. I then converted the signal so that it could be read out on a television monitor. Sure enough, it was the same Channel 25 and I could see it on the screen. This guy was actually intercepting Channel 25 from Brooklyn and rebroadcasting it. His implant was on the same exact frequency, but there was also a bizarre technical oddity at work. This implant transceiver was acting in the manner of what is known as a simplex repeater. This is a device which has a receiver that receives the signal. There is then a delay after which the signal is transmitted. It is called a repeater because it repeats the signal. The man's implant was perplexing because the

Chapter Eighteen — Implants 103

receiver and transmitter were on at the same time. This may not sound like anything unusual to the average reader, but as an electronics expert I was amazed. I had never seen such a device nor do I know how to construct one.

After I thought about this for a while, I realized that someone had set up an ingenious system. They were actually piggybacking their implant transmissions on Channel 25. If anyone were to get close to him with a radio sniffer and pick up the signal, they would automatically assume it is Channel 25 and think nothing of it as the fellow spends most of his time in that region. Video information travels along what is called a synchronized pulse. More specifically, it travels above the pulse. The ingenious aspect of this particular implant transmission was that it went in a downward direction below the pulse. They were piggybacking the transmission by using another aspect of the pulse to carry their information on it. This is clandestine broadcasting at its best.

After this fellow realized that he possessed some sort of transceiver implant in his body, he volunteered to be X-rayed. Although several different X-rays were done, no implant was found. An MRI done on him revealed a sack of tissue that existed where it shouldn't be. It was simply a fatty deposit. That was all the doctor had to say about it. The fatty deposit was directly connected to blood vessels. Realizing that blood is a saline solution which acts as a good conductor, the pattern was all too clear. The blood vessels ran right through his groin area which acted as the antenna for the implant. It was powered biologically and for all practical purposes was alive.

There is another class of implant surfacing, part of which acts like a portable computer and sits under the breast bone in the center of the chest. Over the heart on the left side, just at the breast bone, you will sometimes find a chip. This acts as the CPU or Central Processing Unit of the implant. It stores the memory and programs to be activated. At the bottom of the rib cage is the biological implant which is the transceiver. It receives signals and sends them to the CPU chip at the top of the ribs. All of these are connected by an incredibly thin wire to another chip at the base of the neck. This is the neural interface which connects to the spine and the brain.

This implant is organized by a group of five electrodes for each nerve. As the nerve impulse travels down the neuron, one electrode will sense it. Another one will cancel the impulse. A third will reinsert the previous nerve impulse or a brand new one. The other two electrodes I referred to are simply reverse directions designed to nullify the impulses already described. In this way, the entire "neural-net" can be accessed and the implant is fully accessible to the motor functions of a human being. It is all very sophisticated.

Additional research has shown that broadcasts in the HF (High Frequency) region reveal a pulse with fuzzy renditions which resemble patterns indicated by the neurological information just mentioned. This may be the signal used to transmit to this particular style of implant, but I am not absolutely sure at this point.

The reason this implant was not previously discovered was that it will shut down if you attempt to probe the neural-net in an attempt to find it. I fortunately came across a young fellow where it was apparently malfunctioning and didn't shut off. I immediately scanned for the implant and found a group of implants. To my surprise, I discovered that I was able to interface with the implants straight to the CPU through an empathic function that just happen to respond to the codes I knew from Montauk. I was able to shut it off, turn it back on, and was even able to scan some of the programming and memories that had been recorded. It was long before I began to remember that I had also designed part of it. I was on the team that engineered it. The implant had been developed at Montauk with my help. This explained how I was able to turn the thing on and off at will. The circuitry had recognized me.

I always like to think that I wasn't involved in such negative nastiness as this, but I've had to face the truth and confess. I was one of the testers and programmers of the Montauk boys. This also brings another issue to the forefront: was I programmed? I have had to ask this question a number of times. My answer is "yes". I was programmed and probably still am to some extent. This is why I work with people and do research. I also have a group of psychics who track the work I do in order to ensure that I am working for the benefit of the people concerned and am not carrying out some form of government program. I am very conscious and concerned about this aspect of my work. Sometimes I feel that I may be the only one who can do this type of work because I'm just about the only one who has fallen out of a government project who is also capable of doing this level of deprogramming. And, if you're going to deprogram someone, you've got to know how the original programming was done. In many cases, I know how to open these guys right up because I helped program them. I would love to have someone who knows these methods deprogram me, but I've been unable to find anyone trustworthy and available who is willing to learn the methods. I also have to be security conscious in the extreme.

There are other implants besides the ones I have already described. For example, there is a whole class of implants dedicated to sensing signals from an exterior location and transmitting back to it. These implants can be located throughout the body but are often found behind the left ear. This type looks like a shard of crystal or black rock with lines in it. It is very advanced technology and is used by the aliens to find their abductees. These implants do not necessarily affect the thinking processes. They are transponders whereby a signal is sent from a home location. The implant recognizes and sends a signal back. With the proper equipment, the abductee can be located.

Every so often these transponder implants are rejected by the subject's body and find their way to the surface. One abductee reported a crystal coming out of his forehead while another saw one come out of the head of his penis. I think that government implants in the genital region are based upon an original alien design. After discovering implants in the scrotum, penis, and vagina, they began to figure out why the aliens were doing this and started making their own. Their next step was to add to the design and make their own implant structure. Where these implants are found in the body depend upon what is being monitored or what nervous structure that implant is supposed to interrupt.

These devices usually look like a rock with most of them being shaped like a tear drop. The sides are straight with half moons on the front and back. They are usually placed in the tissue and left there. At times, wires can be found coming out of the implants which are typically attached to the nerve ganglia. I am not sure what powers these crystal implants have as I've not yet been able to pick up the signals they send.

These are not the only implants, but they will hopefully give the reader an insight into how complex and intricate they can be. Next, we will take a look at how one can detect and clear out an implant.

19
Detecting & Clearing Implants

There are many ways to detect physical implants. One can be physically scanned with the latest technology in magnetic resonance imaging. They can also be picked up with different types of electronic equipment. Perhaps the easiest way is to psychically scan the aura of the subject concerned.

An implant will always create a disturbance in the aura of a person because any object that does not belong in the body will manifest as an auric turbulence of some kind. The aura is the electromagnetic field that surrounds the human body. It could also be defined as the interface between the spirit and the body. Some people see auras as plain as grass. I personally can scan in front of a person's body with my hands and can detect disturbances in the auric field. This will not only reveal the existence of an implant but its location in the body as well.

I realize most practitioners do not have electronic or medical equipment at their disposal for recognizing implants. Aura scanning is something that many people are capable of and can be acquired as a skill by those who are interested and intuitive. You can start by running your hands over a body (without touching it) and simply feeling the disturbances in the electromagnetic field. There are, of course, varying degrees of expertise.

Once the implant is detected, it can then be cleared out. But first, the subject should be prepared for the rising of the kundalini. Kundalini is originally a Hindu concept and is defined as the primal energy or life force in human beings which manifests in a serpent-like pattern.

All energy, including life, begins with spiral patterns that manifest into more detailed and complex forms. This spiral can be seen in the pattern of fire and is the primary emanation. Geometric patterns in nature form around these spirals and eventually develop into biological organs in the physical plane. En route to the physical plane, one will find energy patterns which swirl in vortex-like patterns and form a snake or serpent-like pattern. This channel of energy is known as kundalini which means serpent. It begins in the gonads where the germ of life begins and winds its way around the area which we know as the spinal column. There are seven particular way-stations or energy centers that represent evolutionary stages in life. These energy centers are whirling vortices of energy known as chakras. The first chakra begins in the gonads and is concerned with the immediate survival thrust of the organism. This blends into the second chakra which concerns the reproductive processes of life (sex). The third chakra corresponds to the solar plexus which signifies the survival power of the organism. These first three chakras are known as the lower chakras as they are the baser aspects of life function. Although they are "lower", they are just as necessary to the whole as the higher aspects.

From the solar plexus we move up to the chest cavity and this center is known as the heart chakra. This is where the emotions and feelings are processed by the organism. Ideally, this chakra should blend the lower chakras with the higher chakras. The heart concerns itself with matters of equilibrium. People suffering from heart attacks are often shocked by information which leaves them in a hopeless state of imbalance that manifests as cardiac arrest.

Above the heart, we have the throat center. This regulates verbal expression which should ideally be processed through the heart center. If someone speaks from the heart, they make perfect sense.

As life evolves up this ladder of energy, it next arrives at what is popularly known as the "third eye". This is the area right above the nose and corresponds to the pituitary gland which is the master endocrine gland. This center concerns the intellect and one's ability to visualize and project. If the area is fully unencumbered, the individual will possess considerable psychic ability.

The spiral of life does not end with the intellect but moves to the center of the brain and the pineal gland. This is known as the crown chakra and represents universal consciousness. Energy can be received external to the body from this receptacle that connects to the infinite.

The Hindus represented this evolution of energy as a serpent and it has been gloriously rendered in different forms of art since antiquity. Each chakra is symbolized as a flower that opens as the serpent winds its way up the evolutionary spout. The serpent in the Bible was a symbolic version of this energy pattern which manifests throughout creation. It is for this reason that the snake was sacred to many ancient cultures.

Although I said there were seven main chakras, there are actually an infinite amount of tiny energy centers. I have introduced the concept with seven main chakras as most people familiar with kundalini will recognize that particular system. According to my education, there is also an eighth chakra located between the second and third. This represents intelligence, but it is a rather primal and universal intelligence. It can best be understood with respect to lower life forms evolving initially through sexual reproduction and power struggles. Until the organism attains an intellect, it has to tap a universal intelligence in order to evolve at all. This aspect is conscious but is not very self reflective. I mention it because many abductees are programmed through this eighth chakra.

In summary, what we have with kundalini is a tremendously strong conduit of energy which emanates from the seed of life itself. It is not unlike an electrical circuit which can be plugged into by higher forces and given a charge. This aspect of kundalini tells us that the human vehicle can potentially tap or be tapped by any exterior forces in the entire universe. This is how human beings channel information from different sources usually assumed to be "higher" sources. This is the same principle used in radio and television transmission where the energy equates to waves that literally carry information.

In a typical human being, this kundalini energy is always present but is usually blocked. In *The Doors of Perception* by Aldous Huxley, it is mentioned that our brain takes in every perception that is possible under the sun. If we were to be subjected by all these perceptions at once, we would be bombarded with chaos and could literally not find our way to the next room. Huxley theorized a function called the "reducing valve" which filters our perceptions so that we are only concerned with phenomena that concern our most obvious survival concerns. This cuts us off from a considerable amount of information that is being perceived by our brain. This is the "70 to 90 percent of our brain that we do not use".

It becomes obvious that one could do an entire study concerning the "reducing valve" and whether it was an evolutionary mistake or holdover or if it was doctored so that human beings could be trapped and left in a lower state of consciousness from which they could not escape. Considering the outrageous suppression of information in our society, we have to believe the latter to be the case. Implants and thought entrainment are two powerful tools used to accomplish these ends.

All of this gives rise to the question: who is doing the manipulating? Various factors are involved, but we will deal with this later. Right now, we are immediately concerned with implants or impediments in the kundalini and how to release them.

The Hindus believe that by stimulating the base chakra, energy will travel up the "serpent". As the energy reaches each chakra, it blossoms and opens up, clearing out all the junk that has been accumulated over several lifetimes. As the serpent weaves its way up the spine and opens each chakra, it ultimately opens up the crown chakra which unites with universal consciousness and spills like a shower of energy around the person.

It is the stimulation of the sexual energy which sends it up the spine and breaks the blocks of consciousness. You can consider that each chakra has a block and as you open the chakras, you are releasing the blocks. This approach is actually a combination of Hindu mysticism with modern psychology and quantum physics. It should only be engaged in by someone who has a complete understanding of what they are doing.

Sometimes the activation of kundalini can be quite overwhelming as it takes one out of the normal realm of consciousness and activates all sorts of energies that are disconcerting or unfamiliar. On the other hand, if you don't clear yourself out, you have no hope of attaining a higher state of consciousness. It is really just a matter of reacquainting yourself with the natural energies already present in one's constitution.

Throughout history, it has been said that one can transcend the physical realm through the activation of one's kundalini, but it is a perilous and difficult journey that can only be completed after many years of serious work. Much of the reason for this difficulty is that consciousness has been suppressed. We are now moving into an era when this type of activity can be discussed at the dinner table. The route out is certainly more available, but the path still has to be traveled by each individual. There are plenty of practitioners and a lot of literature on this subject. Each one has to find their own way.

It should be remembered that actual physical implants are in the minority. They most definitely require special handling. Astral implants and mind control techniques can also be sticky but are usually much easier to deal with for the common practitioner. None of the information in this chapter is meant to be a complete treatise on how to clear implants. That would require an entire volume. This is only meant to serve as a general guideline for those in need.

20
Star Wars

Mind control transmissions are another phenomenon that fit in with the subject of implants although they are of a completely different nature. I will illustrate how these work by relaying a real life investigation.

In the summer of 1995, I received a telephone call from a woman I will identify as Susan DaRe. She felt that she had been targeted by mind control transmissions, sickness transmissions and just about everything else. Her story interested me enough to the point where I decided I would visit her and do an electromagnetic study. I was already going to a hamfest (where ham radio gear is bought and sold) in Virginia, and it was not too much out of my way to stop in at her home right across from Fort Meade, a military installation in Maryland. When I arrived, we went out to dinner with her friend Bruce and she began to tell me her life story.

Susan was born in 1951 and adopted by a German family who had come to America after World War II and had been involved with Adolf Hitler's Third Reich. Her family owned a business in the Midwest and frequently played host to intelligence personnel such as CIA and NSA staffers. As a young lady, she had some sort of magical initiation. Susan was subsequently implanted and grew up. Today, she claims to have tremendous psychic ability.

As an adult, Susan searched for her natural father and found out that he had served extensively in Egypt and was very highly placed in U.S. military intelligence. That was all she could find out except for the fact that he wanted to disavow all connection to her.

After listening to Susan's whole story, she told me that she is targeted and that her step family is still connected to the intelligence community (CIA). Susan strongly believes the common theory that the CIA's roots began with the Nazi's SS. She said the reason she is being targeted is the family business. When her stepfather died, she was to be left half of it. Her stepbrother would get the other half of what was valued at about fourteen million dollars. Susan believes the intelligence community, working in concert with her "black magic uncle", wanted to get rid of her so that the natural son would inherit the entire business.

As we drove to her house after dinner, I began the electromagnetic study. I first tuned into an 1080 Megahertz signal that I had been studying for a month. I noticed that when I got close to her car, the signal would appear. When she got well ahead of us, the signal would disappear. It was as if the transmitter for that signal was in her car. I know this was not the case because I'd been picking up this same signal all across the Northeast and it couldn't possibly have been transmitted from her car. There was no question that the 1080 Megahertz signal was being directed at Susan.

As soon as we arrived at her house, I began the electromagnetic survey at that location. I immediately found the 1080 Mhz signal and also found the 435 Mhz signal that routinely emanates from the vicinity of Montauk. I also found a strong ELF (Extremely Low Frequency) broadcast that was as low as my equipment can pick up (about 50 Kilohertz to 400 Khz). I videotaped the entire display of different signals.

The Montauk signal at 435 Mhz was particularly interesting because whenever I pick it up from Montauk, it is usually broken into pieces. If the pieces were put together, it would make up a signal like the one I was viewing in Maryland. As Susan moved in and out of the house, I noticed subtle changes in the scope pattern for the 435 Mhz signal. I had her walk around, and wherever she would position herself, a subtle change would show up on the scope and be noticeable on the receiver as well. Next, I tuned back into the 1080 Mhz signal and tried the same thing. If she sat still in the car, the 1080 Mhz signal faded out. If she moved around, it came back.

Susan then showed me a report by Dr. Peter Moscow. He is the president of the U.S. Psychotronics Association and is an excellent bioelectric magnetic researcher. He is involved with Wilhelm Reich's work and radionics, and I was already familiar with him. His report indicated that she had brain damage and had been exposed to aberrant electromagnetic fields such as ELF and VLF fields. I had definitely picked up the aberrant electromagnetic fields (the 435 Mhz and 1080 Mhz signals).

When Susan had an MRI done, there were sections of her brain where the myelin sheathing was disappearing. This is known to be the start of Multiple Sclerosis. She believes this ailment to be a result of the transmissions broadcasted in her direction. I believe this is possible and I will explain why. First, we will cover what the 435 Mhz—1080 Mhz network really is.*

These signals start out as a particle transmission very much like I described in *Pyramids of Montauk* (this information has been reproduced at the back of this book as Appendix B). The whole idea of a particle accelerator is that you are getting a unit of electromagnetic energy (a nitrogen atom is best for interacting with the atmosphere) to continually increase its velocity. As the particles are converted to the speed of light, vast amounts of energy are released.

---

* 435 Mhz refers to frequencies anywhere in 400-450 Mhz band and 1080 Mhz refers to those in the 1000-1200 Mhz band. Technicians should note that I took extra care to ensure that I was not picking up transmissions from the GPS or Global Position System which transmits at 1236 Mhz and is used by ocean going vessels and airplanes for navigational purposes.

There are about 24 to 36 of these sites all around the planet. Each one of them shoots up to a series of small satellites that are referred to as popcorn satellites. This is all part of the Strategic Defense Initiative (more commonly known as S.D.I. or Star Wars). These beams bounce around a network of satellites all around the planet. Some of the satellites multiply the beams while some of them combine the beams. By controlling the positioning and orientation of the satellites, the military can direct a combined beam anywhere on the planet. They can also defocus it to where it is essentially a particle wave.

There is a very interesting enigma that I have observed regarding this satellite system. The 1080 Mhz transmissions are high enough in frequency so that if the antennas being employed to detect them are highly directional, I should be able to pin point areas in the sky where the satellites are at a given time. The enigma has been that no matter where I point the antenna in the sky, I get a signal that is of uniform strength. Putting this information together with what Dr. Nicholas Begich has been saying, leads to even more interesting conclusions.

Dr. Begich has published information about a project known as HAARP which stands for High-frequency Active Auroral Research Project. This is commonly known as a weather control project, but Dr. Begich has picked up 435 Mhz signals connected to HAARP and indicates that a mind control function is being employed.

In addition to Dr. Begich's research, there is currently a theory being bandied about concerning a hypothetical nonlinear function that will translate one frequency to another frequency. I think that is exactly what is happening in the case of project HAARP. High Frequency signals developed through project HAARP are designed to ionize the energy in the upper atmosphere which consists primarily of nitrogen. The ionized nitrogen (N_2) then acts as a translator that will literally convert the 435 Mhz particle beam transmission into one of 1080 Mhz. This is a rather ingenious development because it bypasses the need for satellites. I believe this to be one of the latest developments of the Star Wars technology.

I began to figure this out when I first encountered the 1080 Mhz frequency and asked Duncan Cameron to do a purely psychic reading on it. After listening to the signal, Duncan said that it is approximately 2.7 times the 435 Mhz signal. This is not far off at all. If you consider that 400-450 Mhz is the window to the human consciousness, you can divide 1080 Mhz by 2.7 and you will arrive at 400. The ratio of 2.7 is a direct hit.

When I ran this information by my nuclear physicist friend Dan, he became excited because 2.77 is the ratio of nitrogen to air with regard to the Earth's atmosphere. In scientific terms, this would be stated:

$$\frac{M_{ATM}}{M_{N_2}} = 2.77$$

In other words, if you divide the mass of the atmosphere by the mass of nitrogen, you will arrive at 2.77. This information was the initial clue that there was a relationship between nitrogen and the 435 Mhz transmissions. Based upon his experience, Dan concluded that we were most likely dealing with a nitrogen particle beam. The above information about HAARP finally explained what was going on.

Dan also talked about a side effect that is produced when the particle beams annihilate each other. He said that when the nitrogen and anti-nitrogen collide, the element of xenon is released. A couple of radionics tests done on people who have been targeted by the 1080 Mhz signal indicated they had a high degree of nitrogen and xenon in their systems. Susan's symptoms were like a nitrogen narcosis, more commonly known as "the bends".

All of this gets even more interesting because Duncan's psychic reading said that the particle beam system can also be used in genetic engineering. I then ran this information by a geneticist friend of mine who found it noteworthy because the subharmonic of the DNA helix is 1100 Mhz. At the same time, another person pointed out a book by a Canadian which indicated that if one created a certain frequency with a xenon lamp, a thought form was created that was healing and regenerative.

The theory here is that one can literally do genetic engineering by using the 1100 Mhz frequency to resonate with the DNA and thereby open and close it. The annihilation of particles (from the particle accelerator) releases a pattern which controls the way the DNA will reassemble itself. The xenon gas effect would be used to regenerate the new DNA. I ran this by my friend, Al Bielek, who told me he has a scientist friend who had previously read the blueprint for the entire satellite network. This scientist told the people at his company that if this system were beamed at the entire population, it would genetically destroy the human race.

Earlier in this chapter, I mentioned the damage in the myelin sheathing of Susan DaRe and this could be the degenerative genetic effect that Al's friend warned of. This may be why we have suddenly seen MS appear all over the country. MS has reportedly increased at least 100 fold over the last five years.

All of this means that the entire Star Wars system could be used to attack our immune systems and mental well being. We already know that 400-450 Mhz is the window frequency to the human consciousness. 435 Mhz is the specific frequency related to the appearance of UFOs. It also manifests from the Milky Way and is thought to be the background frequency of our reality. The Star Wars system, at least part of it, transmits a signal between 1000 Mhz and 1200 Mhz that is derived from a nitrogen based particle beam. This signal is a multiplication of 435 Mhz, our reality's background frequency.

The signals I picked up during this electromagnetic survey were all between 1080 Mhz (2.7 times 400) and 1124 Mhz (2.7 times 416 Mhz) and it is the frequency of 1100 Mhz which is supposed to be the window to the human DNA. I couldn't get the geneticist to tie it down to an exact frequency, so this is an approximation. He said it is about 1000 to 1200 Mhz. A further corroboration of this theory is easy to recognize if you realize that the molecular structure of proteins contain nitrogen as a primary ingredient. This makes the nitrogen to air ratio make even more sense. The appearance of nitrogen in proteins does not contradict the fact that life is carbon based. As life evolves into higher order forms, it develops proteins which consist of nitrogen.

Genetic programming suggests something far beyond the prospect of biological warfare. It includes the possibility of scrambling or rearranging our DNA. This type of thinking is prevalent in certain New Age dogma which indicates that the human race is currently undergoing a transdimensional change. Angels or the like will appear and rearrange your light body so that you resonate with a higher octave. This may be true but it is much more theoretical and other worldly if angels or other dimensional beings are doing it. If the secret government or the military industrial complex has this capability, we are dealing with an undeniable real world scenario. There are many possibilities to consider.

My first thought on this is that the power base on this planet is afraid of giving up its hold on its power. Their interest in controlling our DNA would be to prevent a migration to another dimension. That is why they might be researching this technology. A second possibility is that they are going to help us for our own benefit. That is wishful thinking to say the least.

Another possibility is that this entire project is being orchestrated for some vast experiment. It could be for the good or bad of the continuum. Maybe the bad guys have plans to either do in or at least subjugate the entire human race. At the same time, the good guys or ascended masters are letting it run until they can step in at the last minute and bring us all to the next level. Some variation on this theme is also possible. There are many different puppet masters who could be involved.

There is an infamous island off the north fork of Long Island that is called Plum Island. It is forbidden territory to the media or anyone else and has long been thought to be a center of bacteriological research that includes biological warfare. This was true for many years, but I know that today they are concerned with human genetic research based upon particle accelerators. These accelerators are no secret and can be viewed from the air.

None of this information is included purely to frighten anyone. It is in all of our interests to know the capabilities that can be used against us. It doesn't mean they will be, and knowing about it is the first line of defense.

21

Pleiadians to the Rescue

During the summer of 1995, I continued to track the strange 1080 Mhz transmissions I had picked up in Maryland and noticed they were forming a triangulation between three geographic points: Montauk Point, Block Island and Gardiners Island. All three locations were emanating 1080 Mhz transmissions in addition to being situated close together in a triangular manner. I have since termed this location "the Montauk Triangle" as phenomena has been reported in the area which is similar to that found in the Bermuda Triangle. For example, two small airplanes flying into the area disappeared and were never recovered despite extensive dredging being done to recover them. I have not completed my scientific investigation at this time so I cannot say definitively that it is the same or even similar to the Bermuda Triangle, but it is probably a safe bet.

On one of my trips out to Montauk to survey this triangle, I was pulled into a conference with a colonel who claimed to be in charge of the Star Wars system at Montauk. He knew about my research and was impressed with it but indicated I didn't have all the answers. This man acted very concerned that mind control could possibly be piggybacked on the Star Wars defense system.

According to him, it was for military purposes only. This obviously includes shooting space crafts, meteors or whatever but he didn't tell me about that. If mind control was going on, he wanted to know about it so that it could be reported and dealt with.

I don't know what his actual intentions were, but it is common for secret projects to be multilayered. For example, a well disguised secret project would have a humanitarian front like the Red Cross that would not be held up to any form of ridicule. Behind that, there might be administrative organizations that appear benign and of no possible danger whatsoever. Layered underneath that, you might find a technology that appears to be an ordinary technology like a power plant. After that, the funny business begins. A little investigation would reveal the Red Cross type organization is really gathering DNA samples. The administrative organization is really a covert intelligence operation, and the power plant is really something like the particle accelerator we have just discussed. You get the idea.

If someone were running a project out of Montauk or anywhere else, the ideal subjects to run it would be implanted or duped military personnel who didn't know too much. This sounds like the colonel whom I spoke with. He wouldn't tell me too much but seemed interested that I continue my investigations as if he were hopeful he could learn something.

I continued my research on the 1080 Mhz signals, particularly as they related to the particle accelerator and the Montauk Triangle. Apparently, I got too close. In September of '95, I had an accident in my van that cracked the front of my skull. After the x-rays, the doctor determined that my sinus cavity was in danger of collapsing if I didn't get surgery in the next few weeks. My van was totaled and the investigation I had been doing ceased.

The accident was a mystery to me. I went blank and the next thing I knew someone had hit me. It didn't make any sense. Sometimes the secret government will have an agent create a crash. In these cases, a driver wearing a crash helmet will ram someone off the road or just hit them from behind. This has created trouble for the perpetrators because the patriot movement has traced too many accidents back to government agents. This may sound shocking to some, but it's true. The regular media does not broach upon this territory, but since Ruby Ridge and Waco we have learned the American populace is far more upset with the government than the media would have us believe.

In my mishap, there was no driver in a car trying to ram me, but a friend of mine spotted a government vehicle parked in the immediate vicinity. I was about to undergo the knife and had no transportation, so I wasn't in any condition to pursue a possible conspiracy against me. My friend continued to scout around for me and interviewed a lady in the neighborhood. She had seen a man sitting in a car for some time and had reported it to the police. Upon calling the Suffolk County police, my friend found that no such report was on file. This would remain a mystery for several days.

In the meantime, I was concerned about my operation. I didn't know if I was being set up for implantation or what. My doctor seemed genuinely concerned that I would suffer a collapse of the sinus cavity and be sensitive to further injury if I did not have the operation. I sought out second and third opinions and finally came to the conclusion that the surgery was necessary. I told the doctor of my concern about possible implantation, and he assured me that he would not be party to such an activity. I already knew that he was not qualified to install implants. I informed him that if someone were to try and get to me on the operating table, federal agents would show up at the last minute with their own medical crew. They would flash badges and usher everyone else out; under threat if necessary. To be on the safe side, he allowed me to place a video camera in an out of the way area of the operating room. I installed a transmitter in the video camera so that the surgery could be viewed by a friend of mine at a remote location. I also had friends positioned outside the hospital in the event that suspicious vehicles or persons might enter upon the scene. I aimed at overkill.

I was given general anesthesia before the operation and went out. In this altered state, I was visited by two tall Pleiadians. They stood well over seven feet and appeared in hospital garb. It was a dream-like state, and I do not mean to convey that they were hard physical beings. The Pleiadians told me that I was in good hands and had no need to worry. They said the doctor was a Pleiadian agent although he was not aware of it. He would be inserting a titanium plate into my head that would offer me protection from the particle transmissions I have spoken of earlier. I already knew that a five to six inch plate would be screwed into my head in order to fortify my sinus cavity. The fact that it might offer me protection was a pleasant surprise.

The operation on the physical plane turned out to be routine and successful. I was back at home within a day. After a short recovery period, I was visited by an off duty policeman whom I know. He brought an advanced stun gun with him and had me demonstrate it on him. The gun had three settings that read: "freeze", "stun" and "limp". Under his directions, I put the setting on "freeze", pointed the gun at him and pulled the trigger. The man just ceased to move. I released the trigger and he came back to normal. I did the same with the setting on "limp". He told me not to activate the stiff setting because it would leave him with sore muscles.

The mystery of the accident was now solved. The policeman was showing me that some sort of agent had sat in his car waiting for me to reach an intersection. He pulled the trigger and I went out, losing control of my van. A speeding car then hit me. Blood from my forehead spurted right onto a section of the map demarcating the particle accelerator. Occultists call this a blood warning and I took this as an omen. There is an entire other aspect to the particle accelerator investigation that I am not going to go into. It is more of a political nature than a scientific one, and I will stay away from it until the situation cools off.

Chapter Twenty-One — Pleiadians to the Rescue

What I have said about the particle accelerator can be backed up scientifically. After all, there are not too many people who are even qualified or allowed to speak on the matter. Legislators have taken my work seriously, but they proceed cautiously and surreptitiously. The information that I had recently discovered, part of which was told to me, could have created a political fire, the back wind of which could have kept Long Island ablaze for weeks. As there was a major fire on Long Island just before my accident, I have decided that we do not need another one and will keep quiet for the time being.

The entire situation with my accident portrays an interesting scenario, particularly if you believe in the old adage that there are no accidents. It seems that someone was trying to do me in and that the Pleiadians took advantage of the situation and had one of their agents insert a protective titanium plate across my forehead. This sort of action (using an agent) is not considered to be interference by them.

The above theory was substantiated when I was finally able to take my first post accident trip out to Montauk. When the particle accelerator is transmitting at Montauk, I usually see sparkles out of the corner of my eyes. This time with the plate in my head, I saw nothing. Two of my friends, who hadn't particularly noticed the sparkles before, did notice the phenomenon when I pointed it out to them. It is very interesting to note that whenever they were within twenty feet of me, they didn't see the sparkles either. It seems the titanium plate gives protection within a radius of twenty feet.

The plate is not one hundred percent titanium. It also contains gold, silver and some other alloy. It has holes in certain locations, and a complete study of its contents and structure is yet to be done. There is also no reason to believe that one needs to have it inserted into their head in order to receive protection from the 1080 Mhz particle beam transmissions. Hopefully, my accident will serve as a learning experience for many.

22
The Secret Weapon

There is a lot more to learn about UFOs and their accompanying phenomena.

Never before in recorded history have flying saucers warranted as much attention and publicity as in the last few years. The Bible tells us the end times are approaching. Information is coming forth in floods from many different quarters. There is now hope as never before that mankind will awaken from the slumber of millennia.

Even so, it is obvious that mankind is not working together as it should. If we can get a better comprehension of our electromagnetic nature, we can arrive at a better understanding of ourselves. Then we can better interface with each other and with machinery as well. New and improved machinery can then be constructed that is conducive to human beings and based upon our spiritual constitution. The resulting unification of technology with humanity can heal the Earth, abolish pollution and put us on a course of regeneration rather than degeneration. This is what my research is about.

Despite the progress myself and many others have made, many conspiratorial aspects are still in place. Those benefiting from the massive secrecy of information are not going to relinquish their control easily. If a UFO lands or crashes in an area, teams will go in and pick up every piece of it. They will use magnetic detectors, radiation detectors and anything else they need. The radioactive soil will then be removed and replaced with new soil. Trees will be replanted. Then, a second crew will come in and pick up anything else that looks suspicious. If you go to investigate the area, it will be hard to find any evidence that anything at all occurred in the area. If a crop circle appears in America, a crack unit from the military will shave away any evidence and suppress any communication about it.

Why do they go to all this trouble?

The reason is that any knowledge about other dimensions is forbidden fruit. Someone is gaining power and control at the expense of the spiritual beings collectively known as mankind. UFOs and the sciences relating to it are intended to be privileged information. If outside powers were trying to lift you out of this dimension, you can be sure that the powers that be certainly wouldn't offer any help. In fact, they would be working towards the opposite. This raises an eternal question.

What do we do about it?

Our best weapon is understanding. That means all of us communicating what we know and continuing to research all aspects of the phenomena. Additionally, you should write to your congressman and other particular representatives. Many people in the military and defense industry have been sworn to secrecy. Sometimes this is in the interests of national security and sometimes it is in the proprietary interests of the company concerned. If legislation were introduced that negated previous "security" agreements or simply allowed people to talk, there would be a renaissance of information in America. The exact semantics of the legislation have to be worked out. The Freedom of Information Act was subverted by making it nearly impossible to find anything. There is no index by subject! The main point here is that the people of the United States have not been deciding what is in the best interests of the security of the country. Brand new legislation, as provided for in the Constitution, is an excellent way to attack the veil of secrecy that everyone in the UFO community decries. This, in addition to persistent communication and education on these subjects, is our secret weapon. It will not be an easy battle but grass root movements never are.

23
Returning Home

In the last chapter, I said that our best weapon is understanding. As we research, network and communicate with others of similar persuasions, we can also directly address the "UFO problem" through consciousness. Many people in the UFO field have already made attempts in this direction by disseminating "Christian propaganda". In other words, they use the UFO phenomena to propagate stale dogma which they believe to be Christianity. I think we need to examine the role of religion from a deeper perspective.

If we consider Christianity, what does it teach us?

Through some sort of original sin, we have lost face with the Creator and therefore have to have a go between or savior in order to reach God. This lesson tells us that we are no longer in the domain of the Creator and the realm that He created. The Fallen Angels, Elohim, or whatever you want to call them separated from the Creator and made their own continuum of space and time. In Christian theology, this phenomena is identified as "the fall" which is a fall from heaven or grace.

Since the beginning of "the fall", the space-time continuum that we know as our universe has had to be continually propagated on a repeated and automatic basis to stay solid. This is done through various space-time projects of which the Montauk Project is one of many. I consider Montauk to be the flagship project for two reasons. One, I am intimately familiar with it and it has been the orientation of much of my own research. Second, investigations have indicated that it is the central project of all time. This may sound egocentric on my behalf, and I am not unaware of that consideration, but those of you who have read the books on Montauk will realize that it is a highly unique situation. It commands a bizarre type of attention which is quite different than other projects you might hear or read about. If it is not the central or primary space-time project, it certainly does a good job of representing or simulating the original.

The operators of Montauk and the other space time projects took the original domain and fed it back so many times that an entirely new time line dropped into existence. What this means in practical terms is that the Fallen Angels took the Creator's fabric of original creation and monkeyed with it so much that they created an entirely new reality and one that just happens to be based upon a frequency of 435 Mhz. This is a new time line that is parallel to the Creator's but is only loosely related to His. The Christ consciousness is the interface from the created time line to the original time line. When Christ said "you have to go through Me to get to the Father", this is what He was talking about.

If you have the original time line of consciousness that was made by the Super Being, the distortions and perturbations are going to appear as wave forms around that original line. The whole operation can be diagnosed and evaluated on an electromagnetic basis which is the means the space time projects use to regulate consciousness. This is obviously a complex technical subject.

It is thought that God is a super being and a millennia is just a blink of an eye to Him and those on his time line. We've gotten to the point where "the blink of an eye" has been manipulated and elongated into a drama of ridiculous proportions. What could be termed a simple "thought" of the Creator, has become a pit of quicksand and manipulation within that thought. We have therefore dropped out of the Creator's thought. Original sin could be said to be disturbing the thought of the Creator to the point where we have an alternate creation of our own. It is this aspect which makes the Christ consciousness the sum total of our reality. This becomes quite clear when you realize that we can't access the Creator or even the realm where He exists. We are left to wonder: will He ever come back?

The question of Christ or the Creator coming back to our reality can easily be put in perspective if you think about it being announced on the six o'clock news. This shows you how diametrically opposed the two concepts are if Christ represents the original time line and the six o'clock news represents our reality.

The second coming or return of Christ can be better understood if we consider what I said earlier about the time line of the Creator being parallel to the time line of original sin. Eventually, if only with regard to sheer probability alone, these two lines are going to cross. It is from the geometric representation of this crossing that the Christian symbol of the cross is derived.

Some people want to know if this crossing has already happened or if it will happen soon and this can be a lively subject for debate. Obviously, a two dimensional cross is a representation of one time line being in touch with the other one. One could argue that various saints had tapped into the original time line when they worked their miracles. Christ on the cross represented the ultimate climax in terms of the two lines crossing. Of course, the two time lines very much went their separate ways after that incident.

As it was related in the historical accounts of the Bible, not everyone was aware of the two time lines crossing. In fact, most of the recognition came after the fact and only after it was relayed through the media of that particular era. It is the same today. If we have a crossing, not everyone will necessarily be aware of it. For conventional science to recognize such an occurrence, it would have to come to terms with metaphysics, a very big and broad subject of which regular physics is just a small part.

Metaphysics is a touchy subject for many scientists and today some people who can no longer deny other dimensions like to use the word "hyperdimensional physics". This is just a matter of semantics and should not be taken too seriously. These people are afraid they might be associated with carnival witches or astrologers if they embrace the word "metaphysics".

There is a genuine metaphysical knowledge base which can be fully tapped when the two time lines cross. You can already see elements of this beginning to happen in today's literature. It is like Columbus seeing twigs and birds before reaching land.

The early religious data base on this planet that was correct has been severely distorted by man, but there is still a basic underlying truth which can be understood as we continue to develop and evolve. Pursuing this angle, we can come to understand the true cosmic data base and the original truth.

One of the reasons why conventional science has a hard time embracing any of this is that they are in the hands of the manipulators. They are "created" to some degree and are certainly not acting with a creative consciousness.

When someone has the good fortune to access the original time line, they will find there is no room for manipulators or power mongers. It is a utopia without any need or motivation for war. A secret or formal government becomes utterly useless.

The New Age or metaphysical movement is leading us towards a potential nonphysical consciousness and this is quite threatening to the established power base on planet Earth. If it succeeds, the control group will lose their significance. This is why they are spending huge sums on infiltrating the New Age movement and UFO circles. They are renowned for infiltrating a group and sending it in a direction that will suit the agenda of the secret government. The agendas chosen are almost always materialistic in nature. This is why

Chapter Twenty-Three — Returning Home

you will sometimes see a popular psychic channel attacked in the media. Originally, they were communicating on a real spiritual level. Next, the true psychic source is attacked through some of the invasive techniques earlier described in this book. After that, the person doing the channeling is no longer accessing a pure source and becomes compromised. Big money is charged along with other practices that will offend middle class America. The media then picks up the story and exposes another fraud. You get the idea. It is a pattern that has been repeating since we skewed off the original time line.

The Pleiadians have told me that if ten percent of the beings in this galaxy can become conscious of the original time line, then all beings will follow suit. They say that it is simply a matter of pure mathematics. If this is true, the only thing we have to do is spread the consciousness. I hope it is all that easy.

May you have a pleasant journey on your way home.

PART 2
by Peter Moon

Introduction to Part Two

After reading the incredible tales of Preston Nichols, it is sincerely hoped that you enjoyed yourself and, more importantly, learned something new about the universe around you. The purpose of the previous section was not only to inform but to put to rest once and for all some of the major doubt and nagging uncertainties that people have on the subject of UFOs and aliens. Any person with an open and logical mind should now have a heightened awareness and better grasp of these subjects. Those who still remain cynical at least have to admit that Preston has an orderly and exotic imagination that will not quit. Of course, Preston has not insisted that his adventures are definitive truth. He is open to the idea that some of his visitations or other paranormal experiences might be influenced by his subconscious or be the product of his inner imagination.

Imagination is a very key word in this equation because it is synonymous to consciousness and consciousness is the link to understanding all the mysteries of existence whether they concern UFOs or the miracle of life. In the second section of this book, we are about to embark on an adventure in consciousness that will not only give further insights into the UFO phenomena but will tie the ancient myths of the Pleiades to Preston's theories concerning the original time line.

I will begin our adventure by laying a safety net in our approach to the more bizarre aspects of existence. From there, I will chronicle some of my own experiences with paranormal phenomena that led to my collaboration with Preston

Nichols and the publication of his work. As we progress, a grander scheme of events will unfold revealing the mystery of the Pleiades and the role they play in the consciousness of all.

24
The Psychology of UFOs

Modern psychology began with two major personalities: Sigmund Freud and Carl Jung. Freud was the father of psychoanalysis and found a sexual impulse behind every psychological dysfunction. He resoundingly rejected the paranormal and came into conflict with Jung, his former student and colleague. Jung extensively studied oriental religions and the occult, incorporating what he learned from Freud with his own innovations.*

For purposes of this discussion, we are going to discuss the work of Carl Jung. His most brilliant act was to break down all of human psychology into archetypes. An archetype is defined as a prototype or model from which all other things are made. In human psychology, this means that our personalities can be broken down into basic stereotypical patterns that lurk beneath the

---

* There was actually a third figure present at Freud's institute who, although more knowledgeable than both of these revered personalities, has yet to be heard of in most universities because his work has been suppressed. This figure was Wilhelm Reich who absorbed the sexual teachings of Freud and the occult leanings of Jung and added it to his own research. Reich actually penetrated the human psyche as never before in terms of therapy. In his later years, he claimed to have a built a ray gun that shot down UFOs. He was arrested on a trumped up charge and placed in jail where he died. His books were burned by government agents. Preston Nichols has discussed some of his work in the Montauk books.

surface of our social intercourse. These original prototypes existing within our psyche can be most easily viewed through mythological representations of the various gods. A quick study of the various pantheons will reveal heroes, thieves, betrayers, lovers, healers, poets and just about any basic function of the human psyche. To a Jungian psychologist, the gods are merely the irreducible expression of how life functions. Our individual personalities are a combination of the various aspects. By sorting out the negative archetypes from the positive ones, we can get a better idea of who we are. By then tracing back the various behavior patterns as to why we assumed a negative archetype, we can clear ourselves of it and get along better in life.

Jung studied this subject very deeply and wrote many books. He embraced tarot cards because they offer a strictly archetypal view of life. The tarot, in turn, is based upon the Holy Qabala which is a philosophical system linking all faiths and mythologies in an effort to explain all human experience.

In the last years of his life, Jung took notice of the UFO phenomena that had entered the culture in the 1950s. He not only saw flying saucers but even wrote a book about them. Despite his vast knowledge and a lifetime of study in the occult, he seems to have missed the boat entirely when it came to the study of UFOs. At least he acknowledged their presence, but nowhere did I ever read where he made a concerted effort to categorize the experiences associated with them into archetypal behavior patterns. Perhaps, this function was ahead of his time. Today, it is a much easier task with tales of Pleiadians, Orions and Sirians existing in our popular culture.

The main point I am making with regard to UFOs is that they have to be accepted within the realm of human experience. Whether or not you have had an experience or believe in them is not the major criterion. The fact is that UFO phenomena have been reported upon in vast numbers during the last fifty years. The information can all be reduced to myths or tales that can be categorized with reference to traditional mythology, i.e. psychological archetypes. This means that space people can exist within the context of any reference frame and be devils, angels or something in between. This gives us not only psychological facts that we can grasp when we hear of different UFO experiences but also allows us to study the subject in a sensible fashion without having encountered any hard evidence which is another matter entirely. The psychological or archetypal reference point gives us a foundation from which we can begin to reduce the various lunacies that can easily creep into this subject.

I am well aware that many of you in the reading audience have had experiences of abductions or UFO sightings. Some of you want validation that your experiences were heavenly while others are trying to unwrap themselves from a tangle of trauma. There are also many who, misguided or not, are seeking such contact or are curious about it. Studying the subject of UFOs, etc. from the above reference point and finding out where your experiences fit in will provoke your intellect to interface with phenomena that might otherwise appear to be unexplainable. Where you fall short in your understanding, you can always refer to mythology for some sort of answer. Mythology not only offers a safety net for our study, it is the backbone upon which all civilizations are based.

This is the background from which I tell my personal story. And it doesn't really matter whether what I say happened actually did happen. Of course, I would tell you that it did because I believe it to be so. The important point is that I experienced these events and that they tie into a stream of consciousness which includes yourself. If not, you wouldn't be reading this book. My purpose here is to ignite your own quantum dynamic function in order that you can better recognize your own native consciousness and reach out towards your own unlimited potential.

25

Angelic Influence

Probably the most unique aspect of my childhood is that I was the only kid on my block who was not baptized into the Christian faith. This distinction might have held up for several miles except it stands to reason that there were probably a few others who escaped this time honored ritual. My parents both grew up Catholic. Although my mother went to Catholic school and my father had served as an altar boy, that was the end of it. They were married by a judge and stayed away from the church. Only later in my life would I begin to get an idea of why.

One morning I was having breakfast with a psychic friend of mine and I wondered casually if my father could have been related to Nikola Tesla. She looked intensely at me and interrupted my conversation.

"Your father detested organized religion, didn't he?"

"Yes, as a matter of fact." I answered.

This psychic told me quite positively that a priest had tried to molest my father. She said my father had trusted the cloth (clergy) and it had betrayed him. I don't know if this is true but it explained a pattern in my father's behavior. He ranted and raved against the Catholic Church whenever given an opportunity. He also described the priests as drunkards, saying they would sit around and ask him for more wine after the sacraments. Consequently, I was "protected" from the Church although I was never forbidden to attend. Despite all this, the divine did find its way into my life at an early age.

One day the kids in my neighborhood were talking about guardian angels. Most of these children were Catholic and often told me what they learned in their Catechism classes. On this particular day, the subject was guardian angels and I was introduced to an entirely new concept. After listening to my friends and returning home, I asked my mother if she believed in guardian angels. Somewhat to my surprise, she gave me an affirmative, "Yes!"

Upon asking her why, she told me that I had been saved by a guardian angel when I was a small baby. It occurred on a hot day in Newhall, California when she had put me in a stroller and let it rest under the shade of a large tree. She sat on the porch not too far away. According to her story, a large branch of the tree began to give way. It was not a gradual break and was obviously going to crush me in just a matter of seconds. My mother was too far away to reach me in time and for a split second felt the horror of possibly losing her baby. There was no way I could survive the fall of that branch. As the branch began to fall, a very strong gust of wind appeared and blew my stroller out of harm's way. The day had been very hot with no sign of wind before or after that occurrence. That it was strong enough to push the stroller was most remarkable to her. Despite growing up Catholic, she had abandoned her faith and was not really a religious woman at all, but this experience led her to believe in guardian angels.

I would later learn that a Greek goddess named Alcyone was one of the seven Pleiades and that she controlled the fate of storms and winds. As I have no personal recollection of the incident in the stroller, I cannot say if the above occurrence was celestial intervention by a higher power or just dumb luck. It would seem that some force in the universe wanted to me to stay around for a while.

26
Take Me Out of the Ball Game

My next paranormal experience was in puberty. I was twelve years old and the maturation process was just about to take a big step. I remember playing little league baseball and having a tremendous headache. Every time I would throw a ball or swing a bat, shock waves would go through my system. The normal thing to do would have been to tell the coach to take me out of the game, but I wouldn't do that. In fact, he said that he wanted me in the game and was looking forward to me helping the team. We were mostly a losing team, but that night we were playing the best team in the league and he wanted to win. I was in some other zone of consciousness and figured I would just go through the motions and eventually go home.

It hurt so much to swing a bat that I decided I would let every pitch go by. This decision proved to be more painful because the pitcher didn't throw any balls over the plate and I walked to first base. I discovered it hurt even more to walk than it did to swing a bat. Much to my own surprise, I was batted around the bases and scored a run. The pain was intense. Our team was doing well, but I wanted us to lose so that I could go home.

As painful as it was to swing a bat, I realized that it was less painful than running around the bases. I resolved to swing at every pitch and strike out. This sort of attitude on my behalf was strange because up to that time sports were my only interest in life. There was nothing else and for me to adopt such a mentality was not in keeping with my usual self.

Despite the pain, I swung at the ball and made purposeful outs the next two times up. Much to everyone's surprise, our team stayed in the game and kept it close. By this time, most of the team knew I was acting funny. I was hoping the coach would take me out but he let me bat with runners on base. I went up to the plate with the express purpose of striking out. On the third strike, I accidentally hit the ball for a game winning hit. It felt absolutely horrible. As my team began to celebrate, I hoped the end of the game would bring me some sort of relief. Instead, my stomach began to feel unsettled. It was my father's turn to buy the cokes after the game, and I asked him to buy me two. Hopefully, the carbonation would ease my discomfort. This trick worked just long enough to get me home.

Upon entering my bedroom, I heaved up the spaghetti dinner I had eaten before the game. I completely lost any normal functionality. My mother cleaned up the rather extensive mess and helped me get to bed.

That night was one of the most horrible experiences of my life. I don't know if it was simply a nightmare or an abduction of some sort, but I felt that my mind was being ransacked by a very large and powerful computer. I remember seeing reel to reel tapes like the old computers of the 1960s. It seemed to be probing every possible memory fiber that could exist within my mind and the operation was accompanied by extreme pain and forcefulness. The process was continued repeatedly, and I began to scream louder and louder. Perhaps they were checking out my pain threshold. I have screamed in dreams before where the sound never translated to the physical plane. In other words, people sleeping in the next room didn't hear anything. In this case, my father heard me from down the hall and came in to see what all the fuss was about. He never showed much interest in anything metaphysical or paranormal, but he was fascinated by what I told him

Chapter Twenty-Six — Take Me Out of the Ball Game

and wanted to hear as much information as I could tell him. It was all rather odd.

The intense form of mental intrusion that I experienced lasted only one night, but I found that I could not keep any food down afterwards. After a few days, I began to throw up stomach acid and my mother became very concerned. A week later, she took me to the doctor. He was pretty grim and indicated I could die if I was unable to eat for much longer. The doctor had no idea what was wrong with me. He may have given me a shot of penicillin, but I don't remember. There was no reassurance of any kind nor any suggestion that I could be put on intravascular support. If I couldn't eat after ten days, we were to call him again and expect the worst.

By the tenth day, I could no longer walk out of sheer weakness. My parents and I were waiting on pins and needles. My spirits were considerably raised by the fact my best friend's father, a former neighbor, was coming to visit. I was reduced practically to skin and bones, and I don't know if this friend's presence did the trick, but I was able to retain my food for the first time in ten days. When he suggested I return with him and spend the next week in my old neighborhood, my spirits soared. I was able to eat some more and began to regain a little strength. I soon began to walk a bit. My father was concerned about my going away in such a weak condition, but he was persuaded by my enthusiasm and by his friend.

I took the trip and experienced a complete resurgence of my emotions, inspired in no small part by visiting my old neighborhood haunts. My physical health returned quickly.

Even though I fully recovered, I occasionally wondered if someone was spying on me and could watch my every move. I never linked it to the previously mentioned experience but simply thought it was something everyone must think about from time to time. The thought of someone spying on me didn't really disturb me too much because I considered the possibility to be very remote.

All in all, this experience at the onset of puberty had changed me. It was very unlike me to abandon my little league team and my first love which had been sports. Of course, it is not so unusual for interests to change during adolescence, but my shift in behavior and interests was accompanied by a rather forceful intrusion upon my consciousness.

27
Missing Time

Three years after the abduction incident, I moved to another town and was socially displaced. Having no friends for about a year, I discovered science fiction and other literature which is designed to open up the higher aspects of the mind.

The most influential works I studied during this time period were the novels of Hermann Hesse, a German mystery school initiate. This path climaxed when I read a book entitled *The Master Game* by Dr. Robert S. de Ropp, a biochemist who was also an occultist. This book described the fact that there were different games in life. I don't remember exactly how he categorized them, but they were rather funny. There was the "hog in trough" game for people who were only concerned with their immediate subsistence and had no time or consciousness for anything else. Just above this was "cock on dunghill" which referred to ego driven individuals who like to gloat in the glory of their own fame. This game could apply to gurus who lead people about or even a boss of a small office who gets off on his own power and the admiration he needs from others. There were other categories I do not recall, but at the top of the list was what he called the master game. This was the game of all games and included the objective of reaching your total potential.

Several initiations began at this point which were of a deeply personal nature and culminated in me making a total commitment to increasing my awareness to its full potential. At this point, I quickly discovered there were two major taboos in society. One was obviously sex as the sexual revolution was getting a lot of media play in those days. That didn't require any great powers of observation. The second taboo, considerably more important, was the taboo on becoming more aware. I found that people could not even discuss the subject with any degree of objectivity. Programmed thought abounded in the society (and still does) and it wasn't very encouraging.

Two important truths I learned during this time period have served me incredibly well. First, all proper path work or initiation work begins from the heart. In other words, you should not engage in any activities that you don't really believe in. For me, this eliminated just about any possible career. The second truth was that your only true teacher is yourself. Alan Watts, in a book titled *Psychotherapy East and West* explained that gurus and Zen masters had been a noble tradition in the orient as far back as anyone could remember. He also said that the culture expectation for these masters was that they were all fakes. Part of this expectation also included the fact that most people would seek them out in spite of their potential for fakery. Ultimately, they would discover the charade. This observation was further modified by the character of the different masters. Some were at least more ethical than others or were more compatible with particular pupils. One could learn something from a teacher but the lessons could not be properly learned unless you experienced them yourself. This was a wonderful warning then and still applies today. Gurus are a load of crap. Once you know the ground rules, you can interface with them and possibly learn something. If you know this, at least you can't complain later that you were fooled. You alone are the master of your own fate.

Another point taught by de Ropp is that each one needs to generate his own magnetic center in order to find like

Chapter Twenty-Seven — Missing Time

minds and compatible groups through which one can learn. Although I lived in a hippie laden community at this point, most of these people were too drug oriented to seriously consider real consciousness exploration. I wrote to de Ropp in hopes of finding some method of accelerating my learning and evolutionary process. He didn't live too far away.

His reply was most interesting. He told me to finish school, decide on a career and apply for admission to the League. This was a reference to Hermann Hesse's mystical group mentioned in Journey to the East. This appeared to be great gamesmanship on his part, but it was also practical advice and sincerely offered. I asked him further questions and he referred me to a man in San Francisco whose family supposedly had a long tradition of serving "The League". I was interested in pursuing all this from a strictly esoteric angle. Little did I know that this man's family was tied to the UFO field, but I did not find this out until many years later. This particular family also carries a lineage that is tied to the Montauk Indians. I am not at liberty right now to reveal the family's name as it could possibly hamper some of their unfinished business.

All of this was a rather interesting line of endeavor to pursue, but it would be interrupted by a new adventure for me. That was Scientology, a word that evokes a definite emotional response to all who have heard something about it. Before I say anything further about that subject, it should be understood that I have not been actively involved with Scientology organizations for over twelve years. I do not rant and rave against them nor do I rah rah their PR lines. I can maintain objectivity on this subject which in my experience is practically an unheard of capability. It would require an entire book to properly represent all my experiences in the proper context and that would be very difficult indeed. Scientology is basically simple but it requires indoctrination and an understanding of its own language to be properly understood. For an outsider to properly understand it, he or she has to become an insider. I will therefore cut things to extreme simplicity and tell you only a few salient points.

Scientology means "to know in the deepest sense of the word". It comes from the root scio which means to know or to cleave. Cleave means to cut but it also means to differentiate. The basic definition of the word and ultimate goal is the same as the Gnostics (deriving from Gnosis which likewise means "to know in the fullest sense of the word", but they go about it in a totally different manner.

If Scientology is properly studied and applied and one does not have unrealistic expectations, one can learn a considerable amount about oneself and how to interface with the universe. This includes a reconciliation of one's past lives and complete freedom from mental and emotional impediments. It is also not uncommon for Scientologists to cure themselves of chronic physical conditions or to awaken paranormal abilities. Scientology also offers valid drug rehabilitation and teaches basic reading skills plus a host of many other things. The politics of the organization were always designed to be separate from the procedural technology employed by the organization.

The entire goal of Scientology processing (also called auditing or counseling) is to raise a person's tone (which refers to their emotional character or quality) and to free them spiritually. It is approached on a gradient scale so that under ideal conditions, one starts out achieving a little and ends up reaching for the sun, moon and stars.

In my first year in Scientology, I experienced telepathy, psychic premonitions and even a complete out of body experience with full visual perception. A few months later, I had joined L. Ron Hubbard's elite Sea Organization which was totally dedicated to establishing high functioning Dianetics and Scientology organizations across the planet. High functioning meant that there would be no adversity with the press, public or anyone else. It was understood that Scientology, properly applied, would alleviate any such bad karma.

After one month in that organization, I found myself on an airplane headed to an unknown destination. I would report to an apartment in Madrid and from there be prepared for a rendezvous with the yacht Apollo, the home and research center of L. Ron Hubbard. It was all very James Bondish. From Madrid, I was put on a plane to Casablanca in Morocco where I boarded the ship longer than a football field that housed 350-400 people. Hubbard was a relentless worker and didn't meet with the various individuals who came aboard. A guide was assigned to me after I boarded, and he gave me a complete tour of the ship. I got several glimpses of Hubbard. One of the first questions I asked my guide was if they ever encountered any UFOs while they were sailing. He was a former Buckingham Palace guard and was very meticulous about his answers. Having been aboard the ship practically since its inception, he carefully scanned his memory.

"Only once," he said. "One time at sea, someone on the bridge had spotted a couple of flying saucers in the night sky. He turned to the Commodore (referring to Hubbard) and asked if he saw what was in the sky."

He said that Hubbard shot back immediately without any hesitation and said, "Flying them quite badly, aren't they?"

Hubbard was quick like that and his range of perception was wide. One heard countless anecdotes like this when aboard the ship, but no one collected them for posterity. Critics of Scientology have always blasted the biographical PR sheets put out on Hubbard by the church and have accused them of being inflated with nonexistent heroics. Actually, the stories reported by the crew on an off hand basis were far more interesting than idealized PR broadsheets and would probably have alleviated the critics to a marked degree, if they believed them.

After boarding the Apollo, I soon had an encounter with Hubbard which probably ranks as the most bizarre experience of my life. Like most new people, I was assigned to the decks and found myself scraping rust not too far away from Hubbard's research room. He snuck up behind me and began "skull watching". This referred to him walking around the decks and "looking" inside people's heads. I sort of knew he was there, but I froze mentally and continued to work. He watched me for some time. His presence was hard to miss. I don't know exactly what happened next, but I experienced missing time. It is very hard to describe, but I will try. It was as if I were in two places at once. There seemed to be a numbness that was blocking my full perception of the circumstances. This was followed by a tremendous brightness and lightness of being. I was elsewhere. Slowly, the idea began to occur to me that I had a distant connection to a body scraping rust. I simply couldn't account for what was happening, but I found myself determined not to turn around. I then heard Hubbard talking with my boss who was working on the sun deck above me. I continued to work. I was still very distant and my consciousness was barely in the physical plane at all. Not until Hubbard left my vicinity did I turn around and see him walking away. Although I spoke of this incident with a few friends, I never said too much about this experience. It was all rather puzzling.

Looking back on what occurred, Hubbard loved to send people out of their bodies if he could. This was sort of a personal passion and in some respects, he considered it his major value to mankind. He was known to have "pierced the veil" of the physical plane. In my particular case, I feel there was some sort of subtle transmission or communication going on which will be explained later on. Hubbard was not only peering into my psyche but was apparently viewing my potential role in the scheme of things. He was obviously not threatened by me or he would have had me scurried off the ship in short order. Although it was all rather strange, it was not a traumatic or horrific experience but just something I could not reconcile until many years later.

28
Through the Vortex

After the missing time experience, my encounters or interactions with Hubbard were of a normal nature, for the most part. I had to learn to recognize him as a human being, and I think that was a struggle for many crew members. There was certainly no way I could easily deal with his own energetic fields. They were tremendously strong and far beyond my reality at the time.

My next ten years were spent intently studying and applying Scientology to myself and others. They also included working for Hubbard and studying his personal history and behavior patterns as best I could. I didn't think anyone who worked closely with him considered for one minute that he was like everyone else. I was interested in what made him tick and watched his actions closely.

To make a long story short, let me just say that I had all sorts of wonderful experiences, including what Hubbard termed "the state of clear". Beyond that are the "upper levels" of Scientology which were called "Operating Thetan". "OT I", "OT 2" and "OT 3" stood for different levels one could achieve. The word "thetan" was the Scientology word for spirit; "thetan" being derived from "theta", the Greek letter which also designates life or life force. With regard to these upper levels, I want to point out something I feel is very important and more than ironic.

From time to time, the media has had a field day with the upper levels of Scientology. The Church of Scientology considers them sacred scripture and that they should remain confidential to the general public and their own parishioners until such time that these individuals are ready to receive them. Both ABC's *Nightline* and the *Los Angeles Times* have blurted this information to the public and have relayed it in a most uncomplimentary fashion. They have reduced the information and transmuted it into a lower form that makes it appear utterly absurd and ridiculous. Scientologists would tell you that it is presented totally out of context. Without adding my own opinion as to the relative truth of this information, I can assure you that the Scientologists are correct in this manner. It has been presented in a fashion that is out of context with what Scientologists believe and practice.

If you study books that are critical about Scientology, you can read different reports on and transcripts of these upper levels. According to this information, "OT 3" is considered to be one of the heaviest levels which deals with lifting a series of implants that have been layered into spiritual beings on a wholesale basis. All of these implants are traced back to a major implant that all spiritual beings have suffered which goes back some four quadrillion years. This implant consisted of a series of loud snapping noises with a cherub blowing a horn, coming close and fading away.* Not too much is said about it other than it was the beginning of time. Those who are familiar with the Bible will recognize that cherubs guarded the gate to the Garden of Eden. Hubbard had apparently discovered a route back to the "Garden of Eden" which Preston Nichols has identified as the original time line.

People who did this level in Scientology were not supposed or expected to move lock, stock and barrel out of this dimension. They would generally feel as if they had left tons of spiritual garbage behind and would have a deep and penetrating awareness of their spiritual nature and perhaps what could possibly be called the origi-

---

* This information comes from the book *The Pied Pipers of Heaven* by L. Kin, VAP Publishers, Wiesbaden, Germany.

nal time line. After that point, the game for most of these individuals became to help others to experience it.

In my personal experience with this level, I also found that the principal of synchronicity kicked in to a remarkable degree. Things began to happen that made sense although they might make no sense at all to others. There is too much detail that is precarious to explain, but let's just say that I had some major illuminations as a result of my Scientology experiences. All of this came to a head in 1982 when I was living on Cleveland Street in Clearwater, Florida. I was probably doing the best I had ever done spiritually and had reached a level where I discovered that anything I willed could happen. This sounds rather presumptuous, and I soon found there were limitations to what I could manifest. Even so, there was a lot I could will to happen. I observed that what impeded the will and the well being of myself and others was the entire physical materialism that this universe is embedded with. By this, I do not mean the philosophy of materialism but the actual physics of this universe and how it is constructed. I mean, wouldn't it be nice if you could make an auto accident erase itself? Although miracles and remarkable things can occur in nature, willing an auto accident away that has already occurred is not too easy.

I was feeling very good one day in 1982 and felt there were no considerations of limitations in my subjective universe. I dug very deeply and accessed those thoughts in my own psyche which were holding me to this physical plane. Underneath those were a matrix of thoughts which belong to all forms of consciousness. This deeper layer of thoughts could be said to hold the entire constructs of the physical universe together. I then went "poof" so to speak and willed the entire dissolving or unravelling of the physical universe. It was my day off, and I then went about my business with no more thought about what I had decided with regard to the grander scheme in the cosmos. It was all very matter of fact.

Only a matter of hours later, I was standing in a parking lot off Cleveland street and noticed a big electrical explosion in the sky. It was much like fireworks but was very quick and completely bizarre. The first thing I said to myself was that I knew that something had occurred and there was no way I would go into denial over what I saw. The typical human reaction in our culture would be to deny it. I looked around and saw a huge antenna structure near the GTE building. I wondered if there was a relationship. Once again, I experienced the phenomena of missing time. It was all very odd.

A short while later, I saw a Chinese girl I knew and told her I saw something very weird over in that direction. She validated what I saw by saying that strange things occured in that direction all the time. I spoke about it to a few other friends but that was about it. It would take me years to figure out what had actually happened.

My life circumstances began to change dramatically. I was twenty-nine which astrologers will recognize as a major time for change with regard to the twenty-nine year cycle of the planet Saturn. I got married, deftly eased out of my Scientology career and ended up moving to Long Island just weeks before the culmination of the Montauk Project on August 12, 1983.

Years later, I returned to Clearwater to visit some of my old friends. After a game of football, I saw the antenna tower I had recognized years earlier. Pointing to the area, I told my friend, Claude Hensley, that was the location where I had seen an explosion years ago. He already knew the story and as he was driving, I asked if we could take a look. As soon as we got to a vacant lot under which I deemed the explosion to have occurred, Claude made a comment that he had seen a UFO there once. I had no idea he had ever seen a UFO of any kind.

It took years before I could get any kind of answer to the mystery behind the explosion and the missing time.

29
The Secret of Excalibur

After moving to New York in 1983, I began to live a new life. Although the Montauk Project was at its peak, I was oblivious to it. I had been seeking spiritual truth for some twelve years and it was now time to carve out a physical existence. My wife and I were newlyweds and were planning on a family. This would require work, paying bills, etc. After one week in New York, I noticed that my psychic sensibilities were practically nil. I attributed it to the materialism that is so prevalent in the area. I had no idea that transmissions from Montauk could be jamming me and anyone else in the vicinity of Long Island.

As I moved through various career activities, I slowly began to renew my study of spiritual matters. A defamatory book entitled *L. Ron Hubbard: Messiah or Madman?* caught my curiosity. It mentioned Hubbard's admiration of and interest in Aleister Crowley, the self proclaimed Beast who was known as the Wickedest Man in the World. This book was written by a man, Bent Corydon, who had an obvious axe to grind and I felt that everything said about Crowley and Hubbard was designed to alienate people from the subject. It did just the opposite for me. I began to seek out anything I could find on Crowley, including *The Book of the Law* which is reported to be a communication from an extraterrestrial source.

While pursuing Crowley's literature, I came across an old manuscript of Hubbard's that I identified as his lost work *Excalibur*. This was a book that was quite legendary in Scientology. It was supposedly written in the late 1930s, long before Dianetics. It was said to contain the keys to life and death itself. There was a persistent story in circulation that the first few people who read it had died. At that point, Hubbard had supposedly withdrawn it from circulation. When people asked about this book during my tenure, Hubbard always claimed that the manuscript of this work had been lost or stolen many years ago. There was no particular reason to believe he was saying anything other than the truth.

In around 1979, a major project had begun to dig deeply into Hubbard's past for the purpose of a laudatory biography. A lot of interesting information was retrieved from his personal archives and from across the United States. Much to everyone's surprise, the book *Excalibur* turned up. Hubbard was reported to be surprised as well.

The legends surrounding this book are strange. One person has Hubbard saying the idea was a joke and that no such book was ever written. Apparently, in the early days of Dianetics, he ran an ad offering it for thousands of dollars a copy. One didn't know if he was stroking the market and creating intrigue or if he was really just offering the book for an astronomical price. Other accounts have him actually writing the book. When he repeatedly said that the manuscript was "lost or stolen", he specifically mentioned "the manuscript" and not necessarily the hard bound book. Another legend said that only a handful of books were ever printed. Upon examining all available reports concerning the book *Excalibur*, it seems that a terrific smoke screen was created.

I personally knew the book existed because one of my old football buddies had seen it and had occasion to read it. He said that it was a thin hard bound book and that much of the information was in existing Scientology literature. It definitely existed. He also said that the book was taken out of his hands by a person who later turned on Hubbard and had been in charge of Hubbard's biography project. This particular person was apparently quite upset that my friend had seen the book.

The manuscript I found was not entitled "Excalibur" but it fit the exact description of what my friend had described except that it was not in a hard bound condition. It had been written on a typewriter. It became obvious to me that if this book was not *Excalibur*, it at least contained some of the same information.

After discovering this manuscript and glancing through it, I became charged with energy, but I didn't notice it until later in the day when I was in a park. I hadn't even read the manuscript at that point but had only photocopied it. I only remember feeling extremely confident that I was on the right track. Perhaps I had tapped some of the supreme confidence that Hubbard used to manifest, but I can assure you I was nowhere near his level in that department. There was no missing time associated with the surge in energy, but I did wake up the next morning in my friend's house and it took me several minutes to figure out where I was. This was rather odd as I was familiar with his house and had slept there on several occasions. There is a logical explanation for what happened.

As already said, part of the book contained regular information from Dianetics and Scientology, but it was put together in what I considered to be a refreshing and new format. Actually, it was a very old manuscript. Of considerably more interest to me were a long series of geometric symbols that were designed to unlock the conscious mind. I had absolutely no idea what these were about and although I had studied most everything Hubbard had written, I had never seen anything like the procedures he was outlining. For those of you have read *Pyramids of Montauk*, you will recognize the importance of geometric symbols. They have been used by different mystery schools, including the Pythagorean system, to invoke a fourth dimensional experience. The idea is that if you take a two dimensional symbol and convert it into a third dimensional one, you can access the fourth dimension (if you are lucky). This is what mandalas and even some Renaissance paintings are about.

This is what the editor (who could have been none other than Hubbard) had to say about it: "Symbols have often been used hopefully in an effort to unlock the unconscious mind and derive some answer to its terrible power over man. The use of symbols is not new. Their employment with these evaluation techniques is new for here they are solidly backed by an understanding of what the unconscious may be expected to contain."

He further went on to say that symbols are not a thing in themselves but are a code form that can be used to discover reality. It was also pointed out that such symbols vary widely from individual to individual. There were different procedures to use with the symbols, the first of which was simply reviewing them.

Perhaps the download of energy I experienced could be explained not only by the fact that I reviewed the symbols, but I actually drew them one by one so as to have a record. I was trying to save on copy machine costs as there were many symbols and there was usually one symbol per page. At the time, I had no idea I would be writing books and doing future research.

A further explanation as to how all of this impacted my consciousness is offered by the word "Excalibur" and circumstances surrounding it in my own life. I have not told you that one of the Scientology ships I worked on for two years was named *Excalibur*. I still remember the day I told one of the staff Scientologists from my home town that I was going to be working on a ship by the name of *Excalibur*.

He smiled and said, "That makes perfect sense."

"Why?" I said.

"I heard that Ron used to be King Arthur." he replied.

Excalibur, of course, was the sword of King Arthur and that was the connection this Scientologist was making. I never heard Hubbard say that he was King Arthur, but I know he could easily have identified with such a flamboyant figure.

Chapter Twenty-Nine — The Secret of Excalibur

After all, he was from Celtic stock and named his youngest son "Arthur".

Hubbard's greatest gift was his ability to tap the unconscious and the power associated with it. That is exactly what happened when he snuck up behind me and I was unable to move. He was playing with unconscious forces that were invisible to me at the time, and I don't mean to imply that he was goofing around. It is ridiculous to think that a being like Hubbard, whether you think he is good or bad, would exclusively communicate in just ordinary human terms.

Not even Hubbard's most severe critics will deny that he wielded considerable power. We are offered a clue to this power if we examine the etymology and accompanying legend of King Arthur's sword Excalibur.

"Excal" is a transposition of the Latin "calx" which means limestone. The English word "calyx" means an outer covering. Do you know what has an outer covering consisting of limestone? The Great Pyramid of Giza. At least it did before it was defaced over time. The root "cal" refers to measurement and is seen in words like "calculus", "calculator" and "calendar". If an outsider were to examine our language, they could easily get the idea that all measuring sciences in our culture were originally inspired by the Great Pyramid. Even the word "California" derives from a Spanish word for a fabled island. This was supposedly a Lemurian island with pyramids. There is also an Arabic word "Caliph" which is used to designate the successor to The Prophet in the Islamic religion. Etymologically, giving someone the title of "Caliph" is tantamount to calling him Master of the Great Pyramid.

The suffix "bur" refers to "burn" or "light". This all clarifies even more when we consider the Gaelic root for Excalibur which is "Caliburnus". This simply means "fire in the pyramid" or "fire in time", "Cali" referring to Kali, the Hindu goddess of time. See *Pyramids of Montauk* for more information on the secrets of the Great Pyramid.

According to the legends of King Arthur, Excalibur was a double edge sword imbedded in a stone known as the philosopher's stone.* It could only be withdrawn by King

Arthur himself. Although the sword was imbedded in the stone, it originated from the Lady in the Lake.

The philospher's stone is a well known alchemical symbol. It represents the capstone of the Great Pyramid which contains the total science of Atlantis. The capstone was never found and is one of those historical mysteries. Occult history tells us that it dissolved and could no longer be activated, eventually becoming a fourth dimensional umbrella around the Van Allen Belt. In the Middle Ages, this "umbrella" was tapped into by various forms of consciousness and manifested as the legends of King Arthur. It is also sometimes known as "Grail Christianity". The story of Arthur is indeed the story of Tahuti or Thoth, the builder of the Great Pyramid. Christ consciousness is the software that enables us to access Tahuti's gift which is a super science beyond our imagination and gives us the ability to transform the planet. If we are smart, we will use this super science to access the original time line, not go off in lost or selfish directions.

One other aspect concerning Tahuti should be mentioned here. He was known to the Greeks as Hermes and to the Romans as Mercury. His mother was Maia, the most resplendent of the Pleiades who were seven goddesses in Greek mythology who became stars. We will delve further into the mythological significance of the Pleiades in the latter portion of this book.

Although King Arthur was the only one who could draw the sword Excalibur from the stone, it is meant to represent a tool that anyone can use. The secret of the sword lies in the lake. Excalibur is a secret encodement of the feminine force and how to use it. That the Lady of the Lake is in the lake (water represents the feminine) tells us that the secret lies in the feminine force. This is Tahuti's gift. It is the gift of the goddess.

This explains the secret access of L. Ron Hubbard. Although it is not popularly known, he wrote his work in a

---

* It is interesting to note that Hubbard's magical partner, Jack Parsons, is the author of one published book entitled *Freedom Is a Two Edged Sword*.

trance-like state and received his inspiration from a goddess he called "The Empress".

There is another interesting aspect to the sword Excalibur. Earlier, I indicated that cherubs stood at the entrance to the Garden of Eden. The Bible also mentions that they were accompanied by a flaming sword which turned every way. If Excalibur represents the secret of the feminine energy, this passage is telling us that this is the secret of returning to the original time line.

30
Missing Links

While pursuing *Excalibur*, I had been staying with a friend who had Aldous Huxley's *The Doors of Perception* in his bookcase. Huxley was an interesting character who had networked with Hubbard and was even regressed by him in the 1950s. He had received an initiation and a lot of information from Aleister Crowley. Huxley also spoon fed information to Timothy Leary on exactly how to administer LSD to his experimental subjects at Harvard.

The Doors of Perception is a book about accessing those regions of the mind considered a vast unknown to conventional science. The primary avenue Huxley experimented with in this book was mescaline, a derivative from the peyote cactus. He also mentioned other undesirable avenues such as fasting to the point of starvation and self flagellation. The only path that made any sense was sensory deprivation as could be experienced in a flotation tank. This sounded interesting, but I couldn't find one. In fact, the search became rather frustrating.

I continued to study the work of Aleister Crowley in conjunction with the resonant properties of crystals. In August of 1990, I bought a couple of large quartz crystals. I would later find out that August is the time period the Egyptians called the Sirius transmissions. In other words, this is when the occult link between the Earth and the star Sirius is at its peak. I don't know if the Sirius transmissions were helping me via the crystals, but after I bought them and placed them in my house, I finally found what I had been looking for: a flotation tank.

Not only had I found a tank on Long Island, but its owner was the manufacturer of the most modern and desirable flotation tank available. There was also an interesting and tragic tale he had to tell but first I will talk about floating. The tank was very user friendly and had a contour like a whale. There was plenty of room inside with two waterproof switches for lights and music. The water is hygienically filtered and loaded with Epsom salt so that your body is completely suspended in water and completely relaxed. It is impossible to physically relax all your muscles to the extent you can while floating. Subluxations even disappeared through total relaxation. As the tank is totally dark, your mind begins to process information until it finally relaxes and penetrates the deeper layers of consciousness. I not only found it to be extremely fun but it also opened up psychic channels of the mind. At the very least, it relaxes one's body. I soon realized that if people floated every day, there would be a lot less strife in the world and a great deal more productivity. This is where the tragic tale comes into play.

The man who manufactures these tanks is Peter Shepherd. He told me that he used to have a large factory in Babylon and had begun producing flotation tanks at a rapid clip. Suddenly, a few short weeks before a fire destroyed his facility, his insurance policy was arbitrarily cancelled. The source of the fire was found to be lightning. I told him this sounded like a conspiracy even though I didn't know at the time that lightning could be manufactured. He had wondered about it himself as well as the whole karma of the situation. The only thing he could do was institute a lawsuit against the insurance company. Although he suffered severe losses and had to cut back his productivity, he continues to manufacture flotation tanks today.

The reason there would be a conspiracy against floating is that it raises your consciousness. Preston has explained to

Chapter Thirty — Missing Links

me that the black helicopters you see over America contain sophisticated devices that could best be compared to spectrum analyzers. The helicopters go scouting for certain types of emanations and once they see a certain pattern, they or another helicopter will transmit different frequencies into the area. The entire operation is designed to monitor consciousness. I have also found it rather remarkable that if you try to get someone to float, it is like pulling teeth. The most prevalent excuse is claustrophobia. The tanks Peter has are not claustrophobic at all and can be opened by the floater in a moment. Inner space is certainly more boundless than the wide open spaces of Earth. Consciousness is still very much a taboo in our current society.

Actually, there is one possibly valid excuse for not floating which is that it could open you up to psychotronic attack. I have experienced such, but there are also means of protecting yourself. Besides, if you never throw a punch, you will never win the fight.

The flotation experience opened up my consciousness very wide. One month later, on Halloween 1990, I saw my first UFO. I woke for no apparent reason at daybreak and looked out my window. What looked like a shooting star shot up from the ground somewhere from the north shore of Long Island. I told myself that shooting stars do not go upwards. Within fifteen seconds a second "shooting star" shot up in the very same area.

Two days later, I ran into Shelley Dumas, a psychic on Long Island who works with abductees and contactees. I told her about the experience and she simply said, "They wanted you to see them".

The next week, I would walk into a meeting of the Long Island Psychotronics Association. I was not there to attend the meeting but to meet Preston Nichols as I was interested in him as an inventor. I ended up attending the meeting and heard all sorts of lectures, the most notable of which was how the Philadelphia Experiment of 1943 opened up a rift in the space-time continuum allowing UFOs to enter this realm in mass.

Al Bielek and Duncan Cameron both spoke about their involvement in the Philadelphia Experiment and Preston Nichols talked about the Montauk Project. It was the weirdest but most intriguing flow of information I had ever heard. I asked for a book about it all but soon discovered I would have to write it myself with Preston as the narrator. As I drove home from that lecture, an overpowering thought suddenly raced through my mind: "this is why I came to Long Island". Over time, this made tremendous sense.

I did not decide to take on writing the Montauk story right away. There were many foreboding aspects about it and a lot of inertia against me getting involved. There were two major incidents that triggered me.

The first occurrence happened when I laid down around six in the evening and immediately fell asleep. It was an odd time for me to lie down, and I just went out. What happened next could have been an astral abduction like Preston talked about earlier in this book. It also might have been a dream, but if so, it was a highly notable and irregular one.

I found myself aboard a space ship and there was Preston. He had some equipment and said "I've got your signature". This was a reference to the specific electromagnetic frequency patterns that are unique to my person. It is called an "electromagnetic signature".

I was then escorted to another room that was curved as if it was part of a space ship but the interior was rather plain. Plastic type panels were in the background. An older oriental woman sat at a table and had me sit on a chair to the side. She told me to channel and said that I should do it completely in the Japanese language. I thought her directive was absurd as I don't speak Japanese, but she was firm and insistent. Her mental powers were persuasive as I actually began to try to channel. The next thing I knew I was seeing Japanese language characters and completely understood their meaning. I read them and spoke out loud in Japanese. After channelling lucidly for a few minutes, I became disassociated from the entire operation and found myself apart from what my body was saying. I was concentrating on a part of my mind that I believed regulates the function of seizures. Something was going wrong. Realizing that I would experience a seizure if I continued to channel this information, I shut the entire operation down through an act of pure will. The oriental lady looked at me and eased off. She saw that she would get nowhere if she countered my will.

I next found myself transported to a soothing room that looked like a waiting chamber. It was very relaxing. I regrouped all my thoughts and became fully conscious of who I was and where I was. I knew that I could wake up, be in my bedroom and be totally awake in my normal state. I decided to wake up and open my eyes.

The clock revealed that I had been out for less than half an hour. I was puzzled about what had happened, but I was still totally relaxed just as I had been in the "dream abduction". The experience had a positive effect in this regard.

In retrospect, it seemed that I was being tested. Someone wanted to open up my psychic centers and probably use them for their own ends. It didn't suit what I wanted. I felt that if I allowed this channelling to continue, there would have been a trade off. I would have been much more psychic and maybe even have had the potential to become a famous channel, but I would have turned into a shadow of my prior human self. The whole process could even have required institutionalization or something a shade less drastic.

I feel it is important to mention this incident because it shows that these alien characters or influences can be sent packing and that it is your own agreement which ties you to unpleasant alien experiences. You are not helpless.

Upon telling Preston about this incident, he denied any conscious involvement. As he is a portal for numerous psychic energies, someone could have used him to locate me. The pictures that appeared like dreams could have been representations of thought transfers or energy exchanges that were happening in an objective sense. I don't really know the exact explanation, but I have never felt that relaxed after a dream before or since. The only other time I felt that relaxed was after my first experience in the flotation tank.

My next strange experience occurred in a more conventional dream state. I was awakened in the dream state only I wasn't awakened into the physical universe. I was pulled up out of the body where I appeared to be amongst a matrix of tubes and spheres. It was like a three dimensional diagram of the Holy Qabala (also Cabala or Kabalah). I recognized this as the matrix that exists between the spirit and the mind. According to Preston, this represents the immune system. If there is a malfunction in this matrix, it will eventually translate into the physical plane and cause an illness or death. Shoring up this matrix is your best line of defense.

Two female angels began to perform some type of surgery on the lines and spheres. I was informed they were changing my DNA and RNA. I knew this was supposed to represent a dimensional shift.

Only after this experience with the "angels" did I feel confident about approaching the Montauk Project and writing about it. I do not believe these were angels in the conventional sense but energy units or beings that were changing some function in my system. They communicated to my mind in such a fashion that they were most easily identified in pictorial form as angels.

I began to see quite a few UFOs after these experiences, but they were all rather distant and not close. It seemed that any night I wanted, I could look up in the sky and see them. Dreams on the subject were abundant as well. Somewhat surprisingly, I was not very interested in the subject. I was interested in the time technology known as the Montauk Project which was far more fascinating to me. UFOs were a sidelight and boring by comparison. Needless to say, I was thrust into the UFO scenario. My next adventure would lead me to the trail of an organization that is supposed to control that scenario: the Illuminati.

31

Babalon

My trail to the Illuminati began during an intermission of the first lecture I heard about Montauk and the Philadelphia Experiment. Upon asking Preston how he became involved in all of this, he told me that in a previous life, he and Duncan Cameron had been twin brothers who were named Preston and Marcus Wilson. They had been the first manufacturers of crude scientific instruments in Great Britain and had formed a company with Aleister Crowley's father which eventually became known as Thorne E.M.I., the same company which released the video cassette entitled *The Philadelphia Experiment*.

I subsequently searched for any references to the Wilson brothers in Crowley's writings but could find none. I only found suspicious references to a Duncan Cameron and a trip Crowley had made to Montauk in 1918. Not much was said about either, but I began to encounter incredible synchronicities between the Cameron and Crowley families which are discussed in the book *Montauk Revisited*. Eventually, I would discover that the wife of Jack Parsons, L. Ron Hubbard's former magical partner, was named Cameron. I thought this was too much to believe and I sought her out and encountered her under the most peculiar of circumstances which is described in *Montauk Revisited*.

The upshot of the synchronicities between the Camerons and Crowleys was best described by Cameron. She told me that her original name was Wilson (her father's name was originally Wilson but he was adopted by his uncle Alexander Cameron and ended up using his surname) and that the Wilson clan had descended from the Cameron clan. Further, she told me that Hubbard was a Wilson, too. His father, Harry Ross Hubbard, had been adopted and was originally a Wilson.

A couple of years later, I would discover something about the Wilsons that not even Cameron knew. Researching into the genealogy of her husband's family, I discovered that both the Parsons and Wilson families traced back to Catherine Parr. Parr evolved into Parrsons with the "r" eventually being dropped.

Jack Parsons was also a member of the Illuminati which is known in occult circles as the Order of the Silver Star, the silver star referring to Sirius. His father worked for President Woodrow Wilson, somewhat infamous for his role in World War I and for founding the League of Nations. He is also the president who helped give us the Federal Reserve.

If you read *Freedom Is a Two-Edged Sword* by Jack Parsons, you will find that Parsons believed the consciousness of the world was topsy turvy. Consequently, he took it upon himself to invoke the goddess Babalon, the mother of all creation. In keeping with the aforementioned theory of Excalibur, he recognized the true power of the universe to be encapsulated in the feminine energy of the universe. Parsons began a series of magical experiments which he called the Babalon Working, but he lacked one important element and that was a familiar. A familiar is a living creature that a magician or witch uses to carry out their spell or specific intention. It is usually a cat. As Parsons did not have a cat, he decided to use L. Ron Hubbard who also acted as scribe. After invoking the goddess Babalon for three days, Cameron suddenly showed up at his door. She fit the bill and became the sexual vehicle used in the experiment although she was not clued in on the full nature of what was going on.

Chapter Thirty-One — Babalon

At first glance, it might seem a little vague as to what the Babalon Working has to do with UFOs. If we consider that Babalon is the mother of all creation, we have to backtrack to what was said in Preston's section of the book about quantum mechanics and chaos theory. Babalon opens the door to all possibilities in creation without discrimination. She welcomes all, and this means that everything that has been suppressed in the subconscious of mankind is going to come out of the woodwork. UFOs are a prime sample of the unknown. Hubbard's work *Excalibur* was aimed at the same thing: opening up the unconscious. This is the secret of the feminine energy.

It is no mere coincidence that all three players in this working came from the same Wilson stock. The answer to this secret lies in their particular genetic structure. Before we examine this angle, we will first consider the general nature of genetics.

Creation is a process of geometry. This is readily observable in chemistry and biology. If it weren't, mathematics wouldn't work at all. The DNA in each cell contains not only the complete blueprint for the human body, but the entire consciousness and manifestation of the universe itself. In psychological terms, DNA contains the potential for all archetypes and their potential interplays. In computer terms, DNA is coded just like a program and can ultimately manifest any aspect of existence.

When ritual sex is performed, it stimulates the creative processes on a biological level and this ignites the DNA's creative potential. What translates to humans as the sexual urge is based on a biological program to combine one matrix with another so that the vast panorama of evolution can be created. It is all rather fascinating.

In society, people tend to be somewhat particular in regard to whom they mate with. Inbreeding is an example where people lower the quality of creation based upon their own incorrect DNA coded programs. The Nazi's sought to increase the quality of life with their breeding programs, but this program ended up lowering the quality of life and resulted in conflict and destruction. For centuries, most people have just gone about their business and mated with the man or woman of their fate. More importantly, they seldom try to drastically alter the programming because they aren't even aware of it.

Sexual magick is based upon the idea that you can alter the programming in the DNA through the will or projection of thought forms. It is a time honored practice, the entire procedures of which have been carefully guarded and relegated to secret societies. This is where the two major taboos of our society cross: sex and awareness. By themselves, sex and awareness are not all that easy to master in our society. If you try to create more awareness and direction for your own evolution and that of others through the practice of sex, you are walking on grounds that are even more taboo. While either manipulating or consciously influencing your own DNA and that of your partner might seem like a small scale act, sexual magick teaches the art of doing this on a grander scale. In other words, this is how secret societies try to influence the entire evolutionary program. It is a grand old game that has been going on for millennia. It is not unlike Democrats and Republicans raising signs and cards at a convention in order for their candidate to get the most attention and votes. Secret societies try to steer humanity and the rest of creation in different directions for their own specific agendas.

There is another fascinating aspect when you consider the DNA programming of sexual magick. Because DNA is based upon geometric designs, it is open to other realms or dimensions. If you consider a flat two dimensional checkerboard and realize that you can also have a cubic configuration that could serve as a playing field for three dimensional chess or checkers, you will understand there is a fourth dimensional possibility as well.

Cameron corroborated this view in my last conversation with her which was on her final birthday. Although she was very ill, she had been reading *Pyramids of Montauk* which describes the geometry I'm referring to here in further detail.

She said that was what the Babalon Working was all about. Geometric visions had abounded in her consciousness at the time. These stayed with her for the rest of her life and it was expressed in her art work. She said that the book expressed in words what she had experienced in consciousness. My last conversation with her was a happy one. Cameron passed away on July 24, 1995.

If we consider the Wilson lineage, we have to realize that the DNA of this clan, or at least some of them, have a predisposition to the bizarre. This is not so bad in itself as it is the radical factor in mutations which makes new developments in evolution possible. When one of my friends whose surname is Wilson heard this story, he told me that he was received in a puzzling manner when he visited Scotland. Every time he told them his name, the natives looked at him strangely as if they wanted nothing to do with him. He is extremely personable, too.

The names "Wilson" and "Cameron" have popped up with outrageous synchronicity during my research of time travel and secret projects. Many other people have noticed this too. Robert Anton Wilson is a famous author who has written about the principles of synchronicity for some time. He says that once you reach the horizons of consciousness, you will encounter the principle of synchronicity. It bridges the consciousness of where we are in this fixated third dimensional existence to a possible escape route through which we can access the fourth dimension and beyond.

Flying saucers are fourth dimensional chess pieces and that is why Preston found that space went on and on when he walked aboard one. They are based upon geometrical configurations and a different sort of consciousness than what is considered typical "Earth think".

When Jack Parsons and L. Ron Hubbard engaged in the Babalon Working, there was plenty of sexual excitement going on. Parsons was copulating with Cameron on the altar and Hubbard was scrying and tapping the energy. Geometric incantations were used along with symbols, not unlike what Hubbard referred to in the book I had discovered. They were deliberately working with the same energies and some of the protocols that John Dee and Edward Kelly had used during the reign of Queen Elizabeth I (Dee was her court astrologer). An earnest communication had been made with the territory known as the unconscious or the great unknown.

Many believe that the 1946 Babalon Working was responsible for or tied to the UFO phenomena which became so abundant after that period. This was confirmed for Cameron when she witnessed a UFO shortly after the Babalon Working. She said that the sight filled her with an insurmountable joy. Cameron and her brother were working at the Jet Propulsion Laboratory during this period and had seen a UFO while taking a nature walk in the area. Although she warned her brother not to say a word about it, he blabbed and was ridiculed to the point where he had to leave his job due to embarrassment. He ended up working for the Ralph Parsons Corporation, a huge international conglomerate who builds underground railways and cities among many other things.

After this working, Hubbard founded the subjects of Dianetics and Scientology and proceeded to talk about some of the most far out stuff known to man. He spoke about Fifth Invader Force aliens who were insect-like in nature, and he talked about implants as well. He worked out a whole system designed to free mankind from the confines of three dimensional reality. His relative success or failure is an entirely different subject.

Parsons continued his magical work but was supposedly blown up in an accident in 1952. In a bizarre legal precedent, his next of kin (his wife, Cameron) was not consulted in order to identify the body. In fact, she was not allowed to see him in the ambulance or hospital. The newspaper stories were loaded with oddities. In fact, one of them was by Omar Garrison, a journalist who would later be contracted to be Hubbard's biographer. He brought the house down on Hubbard as far as the courts were concerned. It is quite remarkable that he had also covered the Parsons incident some thirty years earlier.

A few short weeks after Parsons' death, UFOs were spotted en masse over the Capitol. Ever since that time, Parsons has been associated with having some sort of hold on the UFO phenomena. When Cameron had Jack's horoscope evaluated by some of the top astrologers in Los Angeles, she withheld the name connected to the chart. After a detailed analysis, they came back to her and indicated that this person would have to be the head of the CIA. Remember, I said earlier that Parsons was a member of the Illuminati.

Parsons was also a founder of the Jet Propulsion Laboratory. To this day, people at NASA refer to it as "JPL: Jack Parson's Laboratory". There is a whole case to be made that he is currently in charge and controlling things from a secret location, but that is not the purpose of this book. If he were a leader of the Illuminati, it wouldn't matter whether he was alive or dead, for these characters do not live by the rules of ordinary human existence. They regulate the space-time continuum through sex, death, taxes, implants, alien abductions and the like.

Jack Parsons may have been a leader of the Illuminati, but it was his idea to invoke Babalon and thereby change the world. It is my personal opinion that he got caught somewhere in between and that his soul will not be at rest until the goddess reigns supreme.

Cameron has also warned against people judging her husband. She once said very wisely that history can't even begin to adequately evaluate a man until at least one hundred years after his death. The jury is still out.

The Babalon Working and its colorful characters continue to surface as a reference point to many different researchers who study UFO phenomena. The legend and mystique will only grow as time goes by.

Cameron also made another interesting comment to me in our last conversation. When I told her I was working on this book you are reading, she said that she had a very strong connection to the Pleiades. It was all about the feminine energy that is also known as Babalon.

32

The Moon

And what of Cameron, the feminine aspect of the Babalon Working?

She was puzzled that Parsons had selected her as Babalon. It took her years to reconcile the phenomenon and she finally accepted her role. In private, she knew she was the secret feminine force that was labeled Babalon but would never admit it publicly. The mystery of Babalon was hers for she was the vehicle that brought about the magick and interdimensional communications. Reporters and curiosity seekers sought her out for years and wanted to know Jack's secrets. I imagine this amused her and frustrated her at the same time. She often stated that none of them realized that her aspect was the most significant. This was not bragging but simply her realization of the feminine principle she embodied.

If we find ourselves pursuing the Illuminati, we find their mysteries wane in comparison to the secrets of the goddess who is the energy of creation. In fact, the secret organizations that seek to control the planet through implants and other manipulations are only successful to the degree that they subvert the feminine. The goddess is the nurturer and gives life to all. The ruling forces of Earth have polarized so far toward the rapacious aspects of the patriarchy that the question of life on Earth continuing to exist has come into question. Man against nature was one of the first themes of modern science fiction. The very phase "man against nature" is tantamount to saying "man against woman". More accurately, we are referring to man against the natural aspects of women.

Fortunately or unfortunately, the most natural aspects of womankind are only truly honored in the age old tradition of the witch. Jack Parsons said in his writings, "We are the Witchcraft." Both he and Cameron were very much a part of this tradition.

An honest and perceptive study of witchcraft will reveal a very strong to bond to aliens and space craft. In popular literature, witches are usually identified as having concourse with spooks, spirits and demons. What are these but creatures of the unconscious? Aliens and UFOs are no different. They are more or less a different representation of the same thing. As spirits can manifest in either positive and negative fashions, so can aliens. The key point here is that when the witch takes the lid off the cauldron, everything that has been lurking beneath rises to the surface. As a witch in her pure state will embrace the totality of creation, there is no denial.

The rituals of old were based upon communicating with the rhythms of nature. The female of the species is structurally more intimate with nature as she is quite literally responsible for the creation of the human race. These rhythms are most visible in the lunar menstrual cycles.

The monthly moon time was the original Sabbath. It was subsequently bastardized into four times a month in order to collect money from people once they had been lulled into ignorance over what the original Sabbath was about. As there are thirteen lunar cycles per year, this number became a reference point and was the basis of the lunar calendar which is a representation of the natural time line. The rampant superstition against the number thirteen in our culture is really just a rebellion against nature. It is also a blatant effort to program the feminine energy out of existence.

When Parsons engaged in the Babalon Working, he was not only invoking the goddess Babalon but was attempting to propagate a Moon Child. Reporters and the like have often called to our attention that this term refers to the Antichrist, but this is really quite misleading. It is only meant as an Antichrist force to the degree it is the opposite of false Christianity. An act of sexual magick does not necessitate a physical child, but it is designed to give birth to another kind of child: a thought form that will propagate the intention of the magician. Parsons accessed a piece of Babalon when he got Cameron to appear. With her, he tried to create an even more miraculous phenomena. It could be said in different words, but it amounted to an attempt to reverse the false time line back to the original time line. The lunar forces could not be denied and Parsons sought to create a Moon Child to unleash the feminine force. The Moon Child is an idea.

The words *moon* and *menstruation* both derive from the same roots. *Menses* refers to the blood flow. The Latin word *mens* signifies both moon and mind. In Greek *men* is the word for month and is the root for measurement (time) and menstruation while *menos* denotes moon and power. These words in turn trace back to *ma*, the mother of all creation. The Egyptians referred to *amenta* which was their word for the unconscious.

All of the above words are intimately related in the language: moon, mind, menstruation. Menstruation was devised as a natural process to let a woman rest and release the tensions of life. This was the Sabbath which traces back to "heart rest" in the Babylonian language. A woman in her pure state can access other worlds during premenstruum and the time of bleeding. It is a time for visions, opening up the psychic center and communing with the cosmos. This was the cosmic connection that inspired the oracles of ancient Greece and elsewhere. At some point, a priest would come along, sequester the "gifted women" from the general populace and ultimately cut off the channel. If women are allowed to take back their power, the subconscious channels of the universe will open up. We could expect to see flying saucers flying in harmonious patterns as opposed to being a headquarters for abductions and implants.

On a physiological level, the design of the vagina itself is patterned after a geometrical shape known as the *vesica pisces*. The football shaped object below at the intersection of the two circles is a two-dimensional representation.

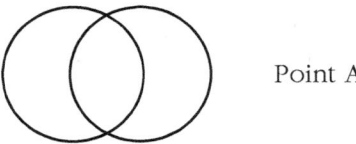

Point A

If you consider the two circles above actually to be spheres, you can visualize in your mind how a three-dimensional representation of the *vesica pisces* would be the shape of a football. There is another interesting aspect to this geometric design. If you look at the two three-dimensional spheres overlapping from the vantage of "Point A", you will see the shape of a UFO:

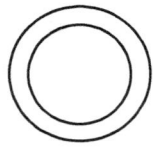

This is not really a coincidence. It is the geometrical representation of two realms or realities interfacing. Christ was symbolized by the *vesica pisces* because he was an interdimensional character who was trying to get us back to the original time line. These geometrical configurations also explain why the vagina has been considered a gateway to other realms by practitioners of sexual magick. Additionally, it gives us a structural overview of what was happening in the Babalon Working. The specific genetic codes of the Wilson lineage made the operation all the more likely to succeed.

The publication of this book coincides with the fiftieth anniversary of the Babalon Working and the dawning of the "UFO Age". Although there is much yet to be revealed, we are one step closer to understanding it and one step closer to the Pleiades.

33
Project KOALA

After Preston Nichols had his initial encounters in the Pleiades, he ended up working at Montauk. This might make the Pleiadians seem foreboding at first hand, but this is not necessarily the case. Preston has been likened in the past to a radio receiver that can potentially tune into any station in the cosmos. If you ever saw his radio room, you would get the idea even more clearly. He claims to have received radio transmissions from the past in that room. As a "human radio receiver", he was also susceptible to transmissions that pulled him into a project that had many negative results.

There were also many time lines involved at Montauk. Reality actually consists of every potential reality that can be conceived and this includes a multitude of time lines. Although their involvement is actually much more complex, it would seem most likely that the Pleiadians entered Preston's reality in this life so that he could break the news about Montauk and raise the consciousness of the original time line.

My own involvement with Preston coincides with the latter. You will recall from an earlier chapter that I experienced missing time in 1982 shortly after making a decision or postulate to dissolve the physical universe. In short order, I ended up on Long Island. It took me seven years, but I finally found Preston Nichols. And, if you're looking for ways to understand the predicament of this universe, he is a very good starting point.

It took me a long time to figure out my own missing time. I even forgot about it for a good while. After returning to the area, I remembered it quite clearly. I asked Preston Nichols about it, but he didn't have any clues. He encounters people with missing time quite frequently. Answers came later even though I wasn't soliciting them.

One answer came after I had participated in a ceremony with Sharon Jackson (as described in *Pyramids of Montauk*), the shaman for the Montauk tribe. Sharon had taken notes before our meeting and had written things about me that she perceived as given from the Great Spirit. She said that I had accessed a realm that had been denied to Preston and Duncan Cameron but that I had been blocked upon coming back to this realm. This same theme was repeated by different sources without them being asked. I then clearly understood that my decision to dissolve the hurtful mechanical aspects of physicality had an immediate impact: my life changed and I ended up in the general vicinity of Montauk Point, New York. I had also made the decision with a clear head and pure heart. In fact, it is probably the most sincere decision I have ever made. It resulted in me being teleported; but to where?

The next clue came from my friend Maia who channels Tahuti and whose work has paralleled mine in many aspects. She told me about a project named KOALA which exists in the future in 8885 A.D. KOALA was established by the Inner Light Network in our current time frame and was projected through a time tunnel to the future. The Inner Light Network is defined as people of Earth who are working for divine order in government and other arenas, many of whom receive direct guidance from ultraterrestrials. KOALA operates on two main levels. The first is human health and ecology to benefit our current time zone. The second is to devise a "code germ" to be entered into the matrix which the extraterrestrials and One World League (code name OWL) have created to manipulate our time grid via such projects as "Montauk". This germ, if successful, would disrupt the gridlock and allow the Metatron* to be restored to our reality.

The Inner Light Network has consisted of such people as Rudolf Steiner and Nikola Tesla. KOALA is the most advanced research center of this network that maintains a black box control center in real time near Golden, Colorado, 250 feet underground in a small complex. KOALA is the counter balance to the Montauk Project, keeping it in check for now and eventually designed to render it powerless.

Montauk, Atlantis and Cydonia (location of the face and pyramids on Mars) were originally a part of the Kali** Rift which is another name for the false time line. Besides Golden, there are other balancing nodes such as Easter Island and Ram-Set which is located under the Pentagon.

While the upper echelon of beings who control Montauk are aware of KOALA and their efforts, they are powerless to do anything about it. KOALA sits in a dimension that is not accessible to them and exists in the future Earth reality referred to as the "New Earth Star" by Tahuti. At the time of the Great Transition (also referred to as the Hundredth Monkey Effect or the return to the original time line), only a very small part of the area known as Montauk will be transported into that new reality.

All of this was quite an earful from Maia as recorded from Tahuti. There is much more to the story, but it goes too deep to tell in this book and would require a lot of study to properly explain it all. While it does not answer every possible question about my own experience of missing time, it clearly is the best theory for the moment.

---

* Metatron is defined as the prototype for the basic constituents or subparticles of matter. It also refers to the full light spiral of matter as opposed to the half light or dwindling spiral of matter. In other words, metatronic energy would be that which is ingested with the full light spectrum or expansive light from the first cause.

** Kali is the Hindu goddess of time who devours all. She corresponds to Babalon and she is identified with the "menstrual stream of time". Her colors of black and red are often worn by magicians as well as satanists.

The minute I made the decision to dismantle the negative physical aspect of existence, I was recruited for Project KOALA. No one asked me a thing. Zoom — missing time. My life situation changed dramatically. All of my experiences would prove to serve as a training ground for my work with Preston Nichols. It is not necessary to go into elaborate details, but one significant example is my wife. I just happened to marry an award winning artist and designer who has made these Montauk and Pleiadian stories "come alive" through her incredible illustrations and design sense. This has considerably helped the marketability of all the books which Preston and I have authored. Not even the top best selling authors in the world get this kind of service because their publishers can't or won't afford her or her peers. She not only does this as a favor to me, but lets me participate in her artistic process. This is just one example of many where I have been struck by either "blind luck" or serendipitous coincidence. We were even born in the same hospital. I could go on and on.

If KOALA did not pull me into their operation, then it is clear someone or something else did and it has all been for the positive. It stands to reason that there would have to be a counter balance to Montauk and other negative space time projects. If not, we'd all have been consumed beyond recovery by now. In ancient legends of the Australian aborigines, the koala bear stands for unkillability as is relayed in the following myth.

Koala bear was an orphan who sought refuge with the tribe but was always neglected. In the dry season, he sought water which was in scarce supply but no one would supply him. Even children treated Koala with bitterness and he cried himself to sleep.

One hot summer day, when the tribe was out hunting, Koala stole all their water and placed it in vessels high in a tree. He even took what little water remained in the streams. Koala then climbed the tree and made magic so that the tree stirred and cracked, eventually growing until it reached the sky.

Chapter Thirty-Three — Project KOALA

Upon returning to their camp, the tribe was distraught over the loss of their water. They soon noticed a giant tree in the middle of their camp and saw their water along with Koala clinging to the branches. When they tried to fetch their water from the tree, Koala would wait until they came very near the water; then, he would spill the water on their hands so they would lose their grip and fall. Finally, two of the tribes best athletes decided they could fool Koala by climbing up the tree in a serpentine fashion. Scaling the tree in a corkscrew manner, Koala missed the men as they went out of position as soon as the water was dropped. Finally, one of the men reached Koala, grabbing him and flinging him from the tree. Although he hit the ground and was beaten by the hunters below, not a bone was broken. The Koala was full of life and escaped to his life high in the trees. Eating the leaves of the gum tree, he no longer needed water, but the humans still stand on guard in fear of his magic.

The above myth is more than symbolic of the Koala's lack of need for water. The koala bear is an opiated animal representing an altered state of consciousness, resting high in the trees. The tree connecting to the sky is symbolic of the tree of life which will be discussed later in this book. The legend also demonstrates that man has been at odds with the higher powers of life. If ever there was a project put together to reverse the work of those who seek a lower consciousness, a more apt name than "KOALA" would be hard to find. It represents immortality as well as the higher aspects of consciousness.

The KOALA theme also fits nicely with Preston's account of the Christ consciousness described in **Montauk Revisited**. In that book, a rather incredible story was told of how Christ turned the tables on the negative Montauk operators. So, for now, until we have a better story or more information, we will accept the name "KOALA" as the code name for those trying to get us back home to the original time line via the Pleiades, for that is where Project KOALA all began.

34
Myths of the Pleiades

This concludes the account of my personal experiences leading to Preston Nichols. It began many years ago as an adventure in consciousness originally inspired by the secret societies of Germany, the roots of which trace back into antiquity. The traditions of these societies uniformly refer back to Atlantis and their home stars, the Pleiades, although very little has been said publicly.

The Pleiades are one of the most striking objects in the night sky. Appearing as seven stars to those with good eyesight or as six stars to others, there are actually over 250 stars in the Pleiades constellation and they all are closely linked in their orbits. In other words, they don't move around much with respect to each other.

Almost all the mythologies on Earth, if not every one, have mentioned the Pleiades in their oral or written traditions and consider it to be either sacred or the source from which life sprouted. Seven chambers in the Great Pyramid were built to commemorate these seven stars. The Arabs and Berbers believed them to be the seat of immortality while the Dyaks of Borneo thought them to be the central point of the universe. South American legends indicate the Pleiades were inhabited by gods who visited the Earth. The Mayans believed themselves to be "the children of the Pleiades".

In the following chapters, I have taken what mythological information is generally available on the Pleiades, dusted it off, and put it on the shelf for easy viewing and comprehension. It is also written in the context of the information in this book with additional commentaries that I feel are appropriate. I will be referring primarily to the Greek and Roman versions as the literature is more abundant regarding these traditions. We will begin with the creation of the universe and then trace the ancestral line, in terms of mythology, that resulted in the creation of the Pleiades.

In the beginning was the void (or chaos) and out of this void arose the creative or generative principle known as Mother Earth or Gaia. As she slept, she gave birth to a son named Uranus (the Greek equivalent of the Hebrew Metatron). Looking at her with fondness, he showered fertile rain upon her secret clefts and she responded by manifesting nature: the birds, trees, flowers and beasts. Together, they had many children but the twelve who were most powerful were known as the Titans. Six were male and six were female. Uranus had tremendous creative powers including the creation of the electron. Astrology tells us that he possesses all the secrets of electromagnetism. His creations were more powerful than himself which was symbolized by his children's rebellion and castration of him. This parallels the fall of Lucifer in the Bible as Saturn or Satan was the ringleader of the Titans. Saturn was known by the Greeks as Chronos (corresponding to Melchizedek in the Hebrew tradition) which means time. Chronos devoured his children so he would not suffer the same fate as his father. This not only symbolized the creation of a time line but illustrated the fact that time consumes all those who dare to live in this universe. His symbol was the sickle which he had obtained from his mother and used to castrate his father. Saturn or Chronos has also been portrayed as the Grim Reaper.

Saturn had a brother, Oceanus, who is the divine personification of the element water. He surrounds the Earth like an immense river where everything is created and eventually returns to die. This analogy is symbolic of a torus (see glossary) or the Van Allen belt which are said to house the akashic records. He fertilizes the Earth through rivers and water.

Oceanus had a spouse named Tethys who was the eternal mother of springs. Together, they gave birth to the Oceanids, a multitude of nymphs who lived at the bottom of the sea. One of the more prominent nymphs was Clymene and she married the Titan Iapetus, another brother of Chronos. Together they fathered Prometheus and his brother, Atlas, who would father the Pleiades.

In the meantime, Chronos had been consuming his children for fear they would dethrone him as he did his own father, Uranus. Instead, his Titan wife Rhea tricked him when he was about to eat his youngest child, Zeus. She substituted a stone for the child. Zeus overthrew his father and became the most powerful of the gods.

Although Chronos himself had subverted the original time line to some degree, his reign was far closer to that of creation than the reign of Zeus. The stone fed to Chronos illuminated him. In mythology, stones signified a repository of knowledge or a series of actions. Today, this would be regarded as the programming aspects of crystals. After all, chronometers are crystal based. After he was overthrown and assimilated the knowledge of the crystal, Chronos repented. While Zeus would become known as Jupiter or Jehovah, he would unleash a reign of terror as never before experienced by mankind. Chronos made his way to Italy where he would become known as Saturn and gave man agriculture. In this manner, he became identified with the harvest and grim reaper as well as the natural cycles of life. He was foreboding in some respects but was a friend to mankind and was always very fair. Zeus was much more fickle in his relationships with humans and was often rapacious in his behavior.

During the overthrow of Chronos, Atlas and his father Iapetus had fought against Zeus. They were among the first generation of gods and were loyal to Chronos. When Zeus won domination, he banished Iapetus to Tartarus and condemned Atlas to bear the sky on his shoulders. Atlas thus became the personification of the geometric matrix that underlies all of creation. As he was bearing the sky (of which his Grandfather Uranus was the personification), he was actually upholding or maintaining responsibility for the original time line. In practical terms, this was a huge burden as the time line had been sufficiently altered. He was thus subsequently symbolized as holding up the Earth. Eventually, Atlas was turned to stone when Perseus showed him the head of Medusa.

Atlas was not really a human but he had human aspects. His turning to stone symbolized the complete fall of man into a frozen three dimensional state and an artificial Earth grid matrix. The other side of the coin was that the stone became a symbol for the crystalline body of knowledge that Atlas had experienced. This arcane knowledge became the rallying point for the civilization of Atlantis which began in part as a rebellion against Zeus or Jehovah. Atlantis was named after the Greek god Atlas.

Atlas fathered the seven Pleiades with Pleione, the daughter of his maternal grandparents, Oceanus and Tethys. Known as the seven sisters, the Pleiadians were named Maia, Electra, Taygete, Asterope, Merope, Alcyone, and Celaeno. After being born, the Pleiades sisters danced in the sky and were very happy. When they felt alone, there was great sadness throughout the universe and the heavens shook. Suitors were called for, but none ever measured up to the free frolicking nature of the Pleiadians. They took up husbands but were never satisfied. The husbands are long gone, but the Pleiades still await, twinkling in the night sky and waiting for the day when their romantic partners will make them happy once again.

As nymphs, the Pleiadian sisters were symbols of fertility who loved to play. The root of the name *Pleiades* means both "to play" and "to sail". May 1st is known as Beltane in the Celtic religion and this is the first day of the year when the Pleiades appear in the night sky. It is a fertility holiday and is popularly known today as May Day. The Pleiades set at the end of November. These dates also coincide with the sailing season in the Mediterranean. The Greeks recognized this period as a time of cultural fertility as well. They would sail, explore and conduct commerce. The disappearance of the Pleiades in November signals the beginning of heavy weather which ends the sailing period.

One of the suitors of the Pleiades was Orion who was a beautiful giant hunter. There are many legends surrounding him, but he almost always exhibited boorish and rapacious behavior. Despite his good looks, the Pleiades tried to avoid him as his ill manners represented the original sin which refers to the skewing of the original time line. The name "Orion" is closely linked to the word "original". His symbols were the bear and the boar as he was a slave to his lower impulses. The word "boor" means a rude, ill mannered or rustic person and actually derives from his antics. Orion was born of a Boeotian peasant. Boeotia was an agricultural province of Greece. The term "boer" referred to a bonded slave or similarly inclined peasant.

The Pleiades were crushed by what happened to their father, Atlas, when Zeus had condemned him to hold up the sky. They were further disenchanted when Perseus, the son of Zeus, turned him to stone with the head of Medusa. Medusa was the symbol of rising kundalini to the point where it became a hideous truth. Because of her vanity and disregard of the higher aspects of life, the truth was unleashed in a powerful current with the kundalini rising in its various strains out through her head and hair. She was the symbol of unrestrained truth that was too powerful to look at. Atlas and the entire grid matrix of the Earth were paralyzed into the condition of the false time line. Perseus himself was initiated into the serpent mysteries and had obtained a seeing eye from three old crones. It was a crystal ball of sorts and enabled Perseus to see the truth. "Per" means "through" and is the root of the word *perception*. This crystal enabled him to see a filtered truth instead of the unrestrained and dangerous truth symbolized by Medusa. Perseus was considered a hero and he corresponds to Quetzalcoatl.

His marriage to Andromeda symbolizes the arrival of the Red Race.

Atlas rebuffed Perseus because he was the son of Zeus. The legend has Perseus turning him to stone with Medusa's head but this is really a hidden reference to the wisdom of the stone or crystal. The stone represents the locked up artificial grid matrix of the planet, but it also signifies the crystallization of the mysteries of Atlas. This myth represents the horrible truth that had already been perpetrated against the original time line.

The Pleiades were so heartsick at what had happened to their father that they took their own lives and were cast into the heavens as stars by Zeus who loved them for their beauty. Here they remain to this day, beckoning mankind to learn their secrets.

35
Secrets of the Pleiades

The Seven Sisters were creatures of love. Their nymph like qualities and inability to be satisfied symbolizes the incessant processes of creation. That no one man could satisfy them only means that their continued vaginal undulations will create further prosperity and abundance to the Earth. That they still await in the skies for their romantic partners and wish to share their secrets means that they are ready and willing to be dealt with.

New age thought has promoted the idea that we either should be or are returning home to the Pleiades. Many people respond to this on a purely emotional basis. It is all rather poetic. The lessons and traditions of mythology clearly tell us that the Pleiades are the key to returning to the original time line.

Although the Pleiades were upset with Zeus for his actions against their father, Atlas, they were shrewd in their dealings with him. They realized that he held the power on Olympus and one of them decided to use her feminine wiles to seduce him. The motivation of this seduction was not to hurt Zeus, but to create a child in an act of love who would carry the truth to all Mankind. The Pleiad chosen was Maia who consummated with Zeus and gave us the god Hermes, known as Mercury to the Romans. Hermes would infiltrate all aspects of human affairs, being the god of commerce, communication, thieves and the occult. Although noted for his mischievousness, he was also a spokesman or ambassador for the gods and was the inventor of the alphabet, music, astrology, measurement and gymnastics.

Hermes was identified as Tahuti (the Greeks word is Thoth) by the Egyptians and as Enoch by the Hebrews. His father was also identified as Jehovah and his mother's name, Maia, is suspiciously close to that of Mary. Accordingly, he is identified with Christ who was executed next to thieves in addition to having frequented their abodes. This correspondence only reinforces the link of the Christ consciousness with the original time line. Hermes also gives us the birth of the Hermetic tradition of mystery schools. It should be mentioned here that the life of Christ as reported in the Bible corresponds exactly to the Hermetic tradition. Whether the story is true or not becomes irrelevant. The account of His life is designed to teach and impart knowledge of how to return to the Father. The Pleiades are a way station. All of this means that the Hermetic tradition is aligned with the Christ consciousness.

Before we discuss further aspects of the Pleiades, I will give a brief description of each Pleiad per the Greek myths. We have already discussed Maia who is probably the most well known and influential. I have noticed that more than a few women are starting to call themselves by the name "Maia" although they do not usually know of the name's relationship to the Pleiades.

The Pleiad Celaeno was seduced by Poseiden or Neptune and gave birth to a son, Lycus. According to one tradition, Lycus went to Asia Minor and introduced the mysteries of Demeter and Perosephone, known as the Eleusinian Mysteries (see glossary).

Alcyone was a Pleiad loved passionately by Poseidon who gave her wide influence over the seas. She is also identified with the winds. Halcyons are periods of calm named in her honor. Traditionally, they occur seven days before and after the Winter Solstice.

Chapter Thirty-Five — Secrets of the Pleiades

Merope was the only Pleiad to marry a mortal. His name was Sisyphus who was condemned to Tartarus where he would continuously struggle to roll a stone up a hill only to have it fall when he got to the top. Merope became ashamed of this union with a mortal and refused to shine in the sky. Merope is the least shining star of the Pleiades. This myth shows the futility of investing in mortal illusions as opposed to eternal truths. It makes one lose their luster.

Taygete was pursued by Zeus but was rescued by Artemis/Diana, the goddess of the moon and hunt, who turned her into a doe for a disguise. She finally gave way to Zeus and gave birth to Lacedaemon whose descendants settled Sparta. Helen of Troy is a somewhat obscure descendant of the Pleiad, Taygete.

Asterope is a Pleiad that historians say is overlooked since nothing is known about her. She is a mystery, and the answer to the mystery is in her name. "Aster" means star. She holds the mystery to the stars and this is the mystery of all mysteries. This includes the various aspects of the collective unconscious that have been discussed in this book.

The Pleiad Electra was also pursued by Zeus but she hid from him behind the Palladium on Mount Olympus. The Palladium was a statue of Athena's father (or Athena herself, depending on which version you read) which she had brought to Olympus. Angered by this, Zeus, threw the Palladium from the heavens and took Electra who bore him a son named Dardanus, the first king of Troy. The statue was eventually recovered by the Trojans who considered it the protector of their city. As long as it stood in Troy, the city would never fall. Preciously valued by the Trojans, the Palladium was kept in the Temple of Athena. Ulysses craftily reached the temple through an underground passageway and removed the statue from Troy. Only then did the city fall.

Troy was set up by Dardanus as a Pleiadian colony designed to teach the Eleusinian Mysteries and propagate the goddess, but the fall became inevitable. Electra was so fond of Troy that she withdrew from the other Pleiads so as not to witness its destruction. This is another myth as to why the seventh Pleiad in the sky is said to be invisible or barely visible. It is also gives us a new vantage point from which to view the Trojan War.

36
Troy, a Pleiadian Outpost

The major legacy of Troy begins with the abduction of Helen which is really a story of the struggle for the energy of the goddess. The name Helen derives from Hel, the goddess of the underworld and the daughter of Loki. Helen of Troy embodies the entire feminine principle. She was not only a descendant of the Pleiades but of Perseus and Andromeda as well.

Priam was the King of Troy. He had a son named Paris who was left to die in the mountains as his sister Cassandra had foreseen that he would cause Troy to fall. Paris was found by a she-bear who suckled him, thus symbolizing a connection with Orion. Paris grew up away from the Trojans who presumed him dead. He worked on a cattle ranch and loved to pit one bull against another and watch them fight. He was extremely strong, considerate and most of all, fair. The word *Paris* derives from the root par which means even or fair. The gods took special notice of Paris because of his ability to be fair and they respected him for this quality.

At the wedding of Achilles' mother, Thetis, all the gods were invited except for Eris (Discord) who got her revenge by casting a golden apple amongst the guests. Inscribed upon it were the words "For the most beautiful". The goddesses Athena, Hera and Aphrodite all claimed this distinction, so Zeus deemed that Paris would make the decision due to his fairness.

The word *apple* derives from *afal* which means "to fall". This apple represents the fall from the original time line just as it did in the story of the Garden of Eden. It is also ironic that the legend of Isaac Newton seeing an apple fall, inspired the laws of Newtonian physics.

The apple of discord did its trick, for Paris was overtaken by the power of Aphrodite and he selected her as the most beautiful of the three goddesses. His decision cost the support of Athena (wisdom) and Hera (conscientiousness and the hearth) who would support the Greeks in the Trojan War. Paris seduced Helen who was an exceedingly willing partner and took her to Egypt where historical monuments to her can still be seen to this day. The trip to Egypt symbolizes the shift of power of the Egyptian goddess Isis from Greece to Troy. Egypt was the source of esoteric power which the Greeks had been tapping for centuries.

An interesting ritual took place even before Helen departed for Troy. Many Greek heroes had sought her hand before she finally chose Menalaus of Sparta. All her suitors had made a pact that they would support whomever she chose. This agreement was sealed through the sacrifice of a horse. The ritual included the Greek heroes dismembering the limbs of the horse and immersing themselves in its blood.

The horse was sacred to Mars, the Roman god of war. The Greek god of war was Ares and he got short shrift from the Greeks who portrayed him as slovenly, crude and generally a loser. The Romans and Trojans exalted him. The horse is significant for two reasons. First, its image was used to destroy Troy in the form of the famous Trojan Horse. Second, a horse in a ruined city in the year 6037 A.D. was a focal point in the Montauk Project. People involved in the project claimed they were sent to the future where they saw a horse on a pedestal that contained some sort of technology.

The obvious correlation here is that the Trojan Horse involved time manipulation, and there is some information to back this up.* Etymologists are uncertain about the origin of the word *horse*. It is really no mystery. The root *hor* means time as is seen in the word *horology* which is the science of time measurement. It is also the root for the Egyptian god Horus who manifests as Montu, the bull god of war. The correspondence between Montu and Montauk is fully discussed in *The Pyramids of Montauk*. The root *hor* also is the derivation of the word *whore* which refers to the mother goddess Babalon, identified as Kali or as the Whore of Babylon in the Bible. She is feared because of her insurmountable powers and potential to devour.

At this point, I want to refer back to my friend Maia (who offered me information on Project KOALA — her Pleiadian name takes on a more obvious meaning now) and include what she said in her very first letter to me. At the time, members of her mystery school were on a project in Greece and Turkey (where Troy was located) where they were "opening old rhombic portals". This what she had to say after reading *The Montauk Project*:

> Certainly I have "experienced" the Golden Horse. THOTH tells me that the horse is a "time marker" placed in a "dead zone", where several time waves intersect. He tells me that the "Capricorns", those time travelers from the age of Capricorn (I have known about the Capricorns for at least 15 years) have placed these markers in dead zones. They are energetic devices containing incredible energy fields, allowing those whose spiritual force is attuned to the Metatronic or whole Light Spiral, to "enter" the marker. THOTH says they are likened to chess pieces in that they contain the moves, the codes of "game playing" in the universal continuum.

If we refer to mythology, we can only speculate on what happened at Troy, but we know that something happened

---

* There is a book written in Portuguese entitled *The Trojan Horse* which is about a time travel project in Jerusalem. Unfortunately, no translation is available at this writing.

that destroyed a great empire that taught the mysteries. The false time line carried on.

37
All Roads Lead to Rome

After the fall of Troy, the Pleiades were not to be outdone. Electra had receded in the skies but the Pleiad Maia came forward once again and took up roots in the Italian peninsula where she married Faunus who was known as Pan to the Greeks. The fact that she chose a horned god was very significant. Her uncle Saturn, who had fallen out of favor with the Greeks, had already settled in the same area and he was helping civilization develop through agriculture. It was a conspiracy to get back to the original time line. Saturn is not only the god of time. In astrology, the planet Saturn is the ruler of Capricorn. This is why Maia referred to Capricorns as time travelers in the last chapter. If there is going to be time travel in the universe, it will mythologically be represented by Capricorn which means "horn in the head". More will be explained on this later.

On the Italian peninsula, Maia became known as Fauna. With Faunus, she had a god son named Latinus from which the word *Latin* was derived.* Latinus had a daughter Lavinia who one day burst into flames as she was offering a sacrifice. Oddly, she experienced no pain. Latinus asked his father Faunus about this miracle and he explained that Lavinia

---
* Etymologists are unsure of the derivation of this word. It is related to *latus* which means broad (flat land) which is close to the Hebrew word *lotus* related to *lot* which means key.

should await the arrival of a splendid warrior whom she would marry. This turned out to be Aeneas, the only Trojan warrior to escape the fall of Troy.

Aeneas was the son of Venus and was raised by nymphs. He was a relative of Priam and Paris but did not take part in the Trojan war until Achilles stole his cattle. Aeneas was a brave warrior whose fearlessness led him into many dire situations where he was routinely saved by the gods. During the extinction of the Trojans, Aeneas went to Mount Ida with his father and a few loyal followers. This included the Amazons who had fought on the side of the Trojans. After the war, he took a seven year journey and stopped at Crete and Egypt where he was initiated into the mysteries. Hera was still trying to vex the Trojans and sent violent winds to hinder his journey but the Pleiad Alcyone came to the rescue by softening the storms.

Eventually, Aeneas landed in the area that became the Etruscan empire which was based upon the Egyptian mysteries. He later ended up in Latinum as king. His descendants were Romulus and Remus who founded Rome which was designed to be another Pleiadian colony.

The legends of this general time period showed another "time god" entering the scene in the personage of Janus. He settled in Italy with a fleet, founded Janiculum and became the king of Latinum. He was the first to welcome Saturn after he had been banished from the heavens. Janus is without a doubt the greatest god of the Roman pantheon which is remarkable when you consider that Zeus, as Jupiter, was supposed to be the greatest of the gods. Here you have the Romans rebelling against the Greek Zeus. Apparently, they needed a new god, Janus, to show that the correct consciousness of time was the issue. It is all rather remarkable.

Janus was depicted as a god with two faces, one heading backward and the other facing forward. This symbolized Saturn's gift to him of "double knowledge" which refers to knowledge of the past and future. Janus was also the divinity who watches over doors because doors have two sides. This has further implications for time as well. Janus was the god of beginnings and the month of January was named after him. The month of January also includes looking back to the past and forward to the future, a New Year's Eve ritual. He was also a god of the four seasons. "Janus" was also the real first name of John von Neumann, the Hungarian scientist who was the time doctor of the Montauk Project.

The Roman rebellion against the Greek gods is far too subtle to be an accident or merely a different cultural inclination. It had to do with the goddess and time. The Greek civilization had begun to thrive upon the arrival of the Oracle of Delphi which was known as a female serpent: the Pythoness. Apollo conquered and usurped the pythoness. After that, it was said that the oracle of Apollo reigned supreme over that of the Earth Mother. After the female serpent was vanquished, the seeds of decay in Greek culture began to take root. The Greeks were known as a patriarchal society and were also notorious for their sodomitic practices which exactly parallels the experiments done at Montauk.

The Pleiadian struggle to put the goddess back on her throne was now underway in Rome. The temple of the Vestal Virgins was established. There were seven of them, the same number ascribed to the Pleiades. Vesta was a goddess of the hearth and her symbol was fire. Every city was supposed to have its own Vestal Virgins who would maintain the hearth and its sacred fire of freedom and enlightenment.

Rea Silvia was one of the Vestal Virgins and a descendant of Aeneas. Her father was Numitor who was the king of Alba. He was deposed by his brother Amulius who insisted Rea Silvia live as a Vestal Virgin so that there would be no offspring to overthrow him. The god Mars was a former Trojan ally and he seduced Rea Silvia which resulted in a virgin birth of twins who were named Romulus and Remus. Her evil uncle Amulius put her to death and threw her body into the Tiber River which was said to marry her. The twins sons were cast adrift in the Tiber in a wicker basket. Fate dictated that a whirlpool deposit the basket on a bank of one of the hills of the future Rome.

The twins were suckled by a she-wolf which symbolizes the bond between animals and the female. The twins soon found other parents and eventually grew to understand their royal heritage whereupon they deposed their uncle and restored their father to the throne. Eventually, they inherited the throne and unified the Italian peninsula. They founded Rome upon seven hills which again corresponds with the Seven Sisters of the Pleiades.

Romulus and Remus settled different hills and debated whether their new city should be called Rome or Remora after their respective names. According to the legend, Romulus had built a small wall around the entire city which was easily surmountable. Remus thought this an absurd gesture and jumped over the wall. Romulus considered this an act of contempt and overreacted by slaying his brother. He later felt remorse (this word actually derives from *Remus*) and gave him a burial with highest honors.

This particular myth has some of the deepest implications in our culture. There are various stories written about these twins and their adventures before founding Rome. Some even have Remus surviving but these versions are very hard to find and have probably been deliberately obscured. The stories of Romulus were often rewritten to suit the political winds of the times. History, even as it related to myths, was a psychological tool used to control the masses.

The fact that these twins were of a magical birth by the god Mars brings to light the colonization of Earth by Mars as is described in *Pyramids of Montauk*. The role of the Pleiades as has been brought out here shows yet another influence. Perhaps more importantly, the most important aspect of this myth is the death of Remus. Romulus went on to rule for a long time even though he had done wrong and knew he was guilty. Their quarrel was all over property boundaries which is a patriarchal way of looking at things. Remus saw the futility of boundaries and was thus representing the feminine side. Romulus slaying his brother was an act of vanquishing the feminine. That he ruled for a long time has its own implications. The writings about Remus surviving were buried as was his personage and namesake. It finally emerged in America with the legends of Uncle Remus, a kindly old Negro who was completely nonthreatening. He and his namesake were only suitable for bedtime stories. Of course, this was a contemptuous positioning of the black race with the feminine energy. The ruling powers didn't respect either one which gave rise to a satirical stereotype which subtly expressed their contempt.

The etymology of *Remus* is one of the most interesting I have ever seen. Practically all words in English that begin with "rem" derive from this myth. *Remove, remiss* and *remnant* are a few. The word *remit* means "to send back" but it derives from *remittere*, to forgive sin. The word *remedy* means "to heal". These words imply that there was a deep sense of loss when Remus died.

Remus had chosen the name *Remora* for his city. In modern usage, a remora is a fish that attaches itself to sharks and fish with an oval sucking disc located on the top of its head. They are known to cling for a long time. This is rather astounding when you consider what happens to a twin when their brother or sister die. The spirit lingers and this is quite noticeable especially when the twin dies at birth or in the womb. Such survivors are often "haunted" by this discarnate being, like a remora.

A further irony can be seen if you reverse the word *Remus*. It gives you Sumer which is the name for ancient Sumeria, featured in *The Twelfth Planet* by Zacharia Sitchin as a historical center for extraterrestrial contacts on Earth.

I saved the best for last. Literally one day before I wrote the final draft of this chapter, a book was sent to me unsolicited which is called *Historical Evidence for Unicorns* by Larry Brian Radka. It says the word *reem* in Hebrew signifies a unicorn. Although I haven't read the book, other sources tell me that the unicorn was indeed a real animal who was hunted into extinction because of the aphrodisiac powers in the horn.

The unicorn is also the hidden symbol for Capricorn. The spiral horn not only represents the rising kundalini but the vortex via the horse which was discussed earlier with reference to the Golden Horse. The horn is located over the third eye. Sexual magick is implied with the horn's aphrodisiac powers. Additionally, the unicorn has been used as the symbol for the Christ consciousness in many different myths. The unicorn is not often portrayed in a down to earth fashion although that is his true nature, being a creature of Capricorn. The unicorn brings us back to another time. Perhaps they are not extinct. Maybe someone has been hiding them and waiting for the right time for them to emerge. In any case, the genetic blueprint for the unicorn still exists in the collective unconscious.

It is quite evident from all the myths of ancient Rome that someone knew about the original time line. At least, the collective unconscious hadn't forgotten about it. Rome was designed to be a balanced city on seven hills. When Romulus established the patriarchy, the Pleiadian or the KOALA movement, whatever you want to call it, had to take a back seat. The way was paved for the Catholic Church which does not accept the concept of a priestess between God and man. Even so, the Pleiadians haven't given up. The Vestal Virgins still survive in modern times. They are real people with a real agenda. It seems the Pleiades will continue to shine until we get the message.

38

The Montauk Connection

In order to fully understand the mysteries that the Pleiades present, we have to consider the sacredness of the bull. We were offered a clue in the legends of Troy when it was said that Paris enjoyed bull fights. Actually, it was his main passion and prime interest in life until the beauty contest came along. Aeneas not only went to Egypt for initiation but he stopped by Crete too, the home of the Minotaur and the Minoan civilization.

The bull was once recognized as a sacred Pleiadian symbol. There are plenty of ancient artifacts, including coins and statues, which link the idea of a sacred bull to the Pleiades. This should not surprise astrologers as the sun is in the constellation of Taurus when the Pleiades first appear in the sky on May 1st. According to the Precession of the Equinoxes, the Earth was under the influence of Taurus between 4,000 B.C. and 2,000 B.C. which gave rise to the solar bull god Mithras and the Minoan civilization of Greece. This was also the period when the legend of the Minotaur arose. The bull fights so popular in Latin countries are a legacy from this ancient period. The Catholic Church, who patterned their religion after that of the worship of Mithras, still labels their highest edict a "Papal Bull" (which is also the derivation of the slang word "bullshit").

The Masons regard the Pleiades to be sacred and placed these seven stars at the upper end of their sacred ladder. In fact, it has been suggested that the origins of Freemasonry lie in the constellation Taurus. Their "T square" is the same as the Egyptian "Tau cross" which is thought to have been derived from the face of a bull. "Tau" is taken from the name *Taurus* and means bull.

The Tau cross is simply a "T". It is a symbol of Hermes or Mercury from which the name "Tahuti" or "Thoth" derives. The "T" is meant to signify androgyny. The "T" is seen as the head of the bull pulling down the cross bar and giving us that traditional cross, sacred to Christianity and many other religions. The bull pulling down the cross bar symbolizes the division into two sexes from an androgynous state. This is the advent of fertility and is the meaning of the bull's virility. The Tau also signifies creative spirit.

According to Egyptian tradition, Taurus the bull was the son of Babalon or Isis (or Maia, the Pleiad). As a constellation in the night sky, Taurus was known as the great city of God, the mother of revelations and the interpreter of the divine voice.

There is also another Egyptian goddess whose etymology is suspiciously close to that of Taurus the bull. It is Taurt, the primeval mother goddess worshipped in ancient Egypt as a pregnant hippo or Beast of the Waters (of space). She was known as the "Mother of Revolutions" because her constellation rotated around the heavens. She embodied the idea of time, repetition, cyclic return, and light in night.

The above reveals an obvious link to the word "Tarot" which means wheel and is said to be the "Book of Secret Revolutions of the Stars and Cosmic Time-Cycles". This relationship with the word "Tau" fits in rather amazingly with the word "Montauk" which breaks down to Mon-Tau-K. "Mon" is defined as god with "Tau" as per above. The "K" is just as important in this definition of Montauk. You will see how it corresponds in the following quotation from Kenneth Grant's *Aleister Crowley and the Hidden God*.

The God Montu looks up as you penetrate his realm and gaze upon the secrets of his inner sanctum in ancient Thebes. His patron planet, Mars, shines through the gateway and reflects upon the geometrical processes which represent the matrix of our evolutionary development.

"K" (the last letter of Magick) is the eleventh letter of several major alphabets; it is attributed to the god Jupiter, whose vehicle (the eagle) is symbolic of magick power in its feminine aspect; it is "the symbol of that gigantic power whose colour is scarlet, and who has affinity with Capricorn, or Babalon". The special import of Capricorn (the Goat) is revealed by its attribution, in the Indian Tradition, to the goddess Kali, whose vehicle is blood.

"K" is also the *Khn, Khou* or *Queue* symbolized by the tail or vagina, venerated in ancient Egypt as the source of Great Magical Power. Magick spelt with a "k" therefore indicates the precise nature of the Current which Therion (Crowley) embodied and transmitted.

Several interesting definitions of the word "Montauk" could be constructed based upon the above. "The revelation of the goddess through her manifestation as the illusion of time" is one.

For those of you who have not read *Pyramids of Montauk*, there was a bull headed god on the cover named Menthu or Montu (depicted on the previous page). He was the Egyptian equivalent of the god Mars, an ally of the Trojans and early Romans. The associations between "Montu" and "Montauk" are not coincidental. In fact, it was Aleister Crowley's illegitimate son, Amado Crowley, who first pointed this out to me. His father had not only been at Montauk but some of his major work concerned the god Menthu.

Shortly after discovering the correspondence between Montu and Montuak, I met a woman who channeled some Pleiadian information for me. I don't even remember what was said except that I had a vivid dream that same night. In the dream, I woke up in an ornate bed and found a gigantic book, trimmed in gold. It was about six feet high and was even more ornate than the bed. There were brilliant metallic letters emblazoned upon indigo velvet which read "*The Secrets of the Pleiades* by Aleister Crowley". Unfortunately for me at the time, I woke up before I had a chance to read the book.

I would eventually find a clue when I read that the founder of the Theosophical movement, Madame Helene Blavatsky, was born on August 12th, the date on which the Montauk Project (1983) linked up with the Philadelphia Experiment (1943). I also remembered that Aleister Crowley had been proud of the fact that he had been born in 1875, the same year that Blavatsky founded the Theosophical Society.

Crowley had something very interesting to say about Madame Blatvasky. She was extremely popular in her day and was subject to extreme attacks in the newspapers. As the story goes, she was supposedly caught red handed in staging false "miracles" for crowds. There were several reports of this sort of thing and you can read about them in various biographies on her. Her disciples have sworn that her miracles were real. Crowley made his own observation about all this. He thought that she deliberately staged phony magic acts so she would get caught. Only in this manner could she get rid of the students and hangers on that were just there for a thrill. The real students would already know the truth extant in her teachings and would be uninspired by any kind of showmanship. It was simply a way of separating the wheat from the chaff. Once the hangers on left, real learning could then take place and the cream would rise to the top. I do not personally know whether Crowley's comments are accurate or whether she produced real miracles. Her scholarship is defintely worth reading.

Blavatsky's *The Secret Doctrine* is about 1,500 pages and is very deep reading. It is not something I could read from start to finish without entering a monastery for many months. I have noticed a peculiar property about the book. You pick up it up and read it when you are ready to assimilate the information in it. If you're not ready for it, it won't even interest you. The book attempts to give the entire rationale for the existence of the universe and how to understand it. As I haven't read the entire book, I can't honestly critique it, but

I would say that it is more than amazing. I have been told that her critics seldom criticize her scholarship but talk about her alleged personal life. Sometimes she has been accused of plagiarism, but this is ridiculous because she is constantly using footnotes and quoting her sources.

The Secret Doctrine had some very interesting things to say about the Pleiades, beginning on page 619 of Volume II. There, we learn that the Sanskrit word for Mars, *Karttikeya*, is taken from Krittika, the Sanskrit word for the Pleiades. This same page gives the account of a Dr. Kenealy who indicates that Mars was the most secretive and mysterious of all religious and astronomical symbols. The six viewable Pleiadian sisters, along with the invisible seventh were needed to complete the initiation into this mystery of all mysteries.

We will examine this mystery in the next chapter.

39
The Pleiades Revealed

The most important aspect of the Pleiades as revealed in the mythology and esoteric information herein is the story of the Pleiad Maia being the mother of Hermes and the hermetic tradition. This is reflected in the fact that the Pleiades are referred to as the Seven Sisters. There are obviously more than seven stars in the constellation, but the mythographers went out of their way to let us know there were seven, even explaining that one had receded over the Trojan War.

The esoteric reference to the number "seven" neither begins or ends there. Aeneas had a seven year journey. Rome was built on seven hills. Seven also signifies the generative principle in Hebrew. There are seven heavens, seven chakras, seven musical notes and seven colors of the rainbow. There are even seven days in a week, representing the original seven days of creation. Not only does the word *Babalon* have seven letters, the Babalon Working was based upon a seven pointed geometric glyph known as the Star of Babalon. It may amuse you to know that the world oil cartel consists of seven major companies who are referred to as "The Seven Sisters".

The entire meaning of seven has to do with what are called the septenary (sept = seven) influences of creation. Before we can fully appreciate the full import of seven, we have to refer back to what I said earlier about the Garden of

Eden being guarded by cherubs and a flaming sword. I will now give you the exact quotation from Genesis 3:24.

"So he drove out the man; and he placed at the east of the garden of Eden Cherubims, and a flaming sword which turned every way, to keep the way of the tree of life."

"The tree of life" refers to the original time line of course, but there is also another meaning. "The tree of life" refers to the Mystical Qabala or Holy Cabala which could be considered a pathway or many pathways to understanding the dilemmas of this universe. In a work of this sort, we can only touch on it very briefly. The reader is encouraged to study the subject on his or her own. The Cabala can best be understood as a matrix or interface that exists between the spiritual aspect and the mental aspects of creation. It has also been identified as the basis of your spiritual and physical immune system.

What we are concerned with for our purposes, are the ten fundamental emanation points of creation that are represented as spheres or sephiroth. These spheres are a repeating pattern that can be found in nature. The first three however are separated from the other seven. The first three spheres are referred to as the supernals as they are above our ordinary plane of consciousness. These three supernals have Hebrew designations of Kether, Chokmah, and Binah. Kether (identified in the Orient as the mysterious Tao) represents the divine source from which all things flow. Chokmah is the positive or male principle (Uranus or Metatron) while Binah is the negative or female principle (Gaia or Mary). As Kether compares to the Tao, Chokmah and Binah represent yang and yin respectively. These primary forces ignite all of creation.

The concept of the "sacred seven" has to do with the different emanations or sephiroth that form the rest of creation; what we know as the universe. These are the seven fundamental reference points of creation that correspond with the seven chakras. If you study books on the Cabala and the chakras, you will penetrate the unseen aspects of existence and see these "sevens" repeating. It is simply a matter of how the universe is constructed. This is the mystery of the "sevens".

Obviously, the above is a detailed study. In this regard, this book can only be an introduction to these mysteries or a refamiliarization for some. For those who want to pursue this study further, **The Secret Doctrine** by Blavatsky will enhance your understanding of these matters considerably.

In Aryan mythology, the seven Pleiades were the nurses of Mars, the war god, who is the commander of the celestial armies. The term "celestial armies" refers to the yogis in heaven and the holy sages of the earth. This equates Mars to Michael the Archangel, the celestial warrior who slew the dragon or serpent.

This can be explained in simple terms if we realize that the manifest universe is constructed with the kundalini system. It is not unlike a particular type of software for a computer. We can choose to follow the operating system or not, but it is there. Common Christian "think" has told us to run from the serpent, but Christ said to "Be as shrewd as the serpent, but as gentle as the dove". When Michael slays the serpent, it is an analogy for mastering these seven principles of existence. He is the master of all yogis and sages because he knows what they are teaching. Michael or Mars is an ascended master in this aspect. This analogy of the war in the heavens brings us to Revelation.

The hidden aspect or invisibility of the seventh Pleiad represents the seventh seal mentioned in the Book of Revelation which refers to the undoing of life as we know it. The esoteric teachings about this aspect of the "Lost Pleiad" indicate that all the occult secrets exist in a bottleneck that can be released or not. This is the mystery of the seventh seal. It has also been compared to that of the riddle of the Sphinx which contains access to the Hall of Records. How and when the information is released has everything to do with returning our consciousness to the original time line. As Preston Nichols said earlier in this book, if enough people are conscious of what is happening, we will graduate to the realm of the Creator.

The Whore of Babylon referred to in the Book of Revelation signifies the entire subjugation of the material world to the kundalini system. In Crowley's tarot, Babalon rides the Beast, symbolizing the ruling principle of our universe. Whether we like it or not, we live in a universe of division that is ruled by the bestial urges over which Babalon presides. It is the same story as Eve and the serpent. All of this is compactly symbolized in the sexual impulse which unites man spiritually with the material.

Aleister Crowley taught what is known as the Left Hand Path which is the unification with the Holy Spirit through sexuality. The Right Hand Path refers to the unification with the Holy Spirit through purely noble methods as was expressed in the Grail Romances. Esotericists are notorious for warning disciples of the extreme danger associated with the Left Hand Path. The trouble with the Right Hand Path is that people pursuing it often fall prey to the elements of desire associated with the Left Hand Path because they have unhandled issues there or have improperly explored it. Students often pursue the Left Hand Path for the wrong reasons, most notable of which are sex and power. In all fairness, not too many aspirants make it to the top by either path. This is why the Buddha taught the Middle Way. There has to be a balance.

Earlier in this book, Preston stated quite clearly that releasing the Kundalini was the way to clear out implants. The Babalon Working, as performed by members of the Wilson family, was a grand scale operation designed to clear out the supreme implant of the universe. It was meant to open up the revelation of the truth and bring the entirety of existence into account.

The bottleneck of information I referred to above is critical. The more information that comes out and permeates consciousness, the more things will change. The powers behind the Montauk Project have their own agenda as Preston previously described. They want to maintain their own position of control.

Chapter Thirty-Nine — The Pleiades Revealed

As far as my own personal investigation of these matters, an interesting pattern has revealed itself. As soon as I encountered Preston Nichols' story of Montauk, I began to find correspondences with 666. This included my encounters with Cameron, Amado Crowley and various other factors described in the Montauk books. 666 is the encodement of the physical realm which is probably best illustrated in the structure of the carbon atom. A single carbon atom contains 6 protons, 6 neutrons and 6 electrons. As all organic life is carbon based, 666 is considered the encodement for life in the flesh.

In esoteric terms, this present work is a graduation to the realm of 777, the code for the spiritual system or connection that lies between organic life and pure spirit. Beyond 777, lies the realm of 888. This is the sacred number for the Christ consciousness. It also represents the infinite. It is not really a realm that you sit around and study because once you have attained the 888 consciousness, it sends you right through to the original time line which is represented as 999, the reversal of 666.

When I made a personal decision to dissolve all mechanical conditions of the physical realm, I was seeking the realm of 999 although I had no idea of this particular terminology at that time. That I had some fantastic experiences is a result of the simple maxim "seek and ye shall find". The connection is there for all who want to avail themselves of it.

40
Lyra and Beyond

There is one other aspect of the Pleiades which should be commented upon before we close out this work.

In his book, *The Masks of God: Creative Mythology*, Joseph Campbell brings to light an interesting artifact uncovered from the early Christian era. It is a cylindrical seal which reads *Orpheos Bakkikos* and has a crucified man with a crescent moon resting atop the cross. Overhead are the seven stars which Campbell identifies as the Pleiades. He also tells us that us that the Pleiades were known to antiquity as the Lyre of Orpheus.

The inscription *Orpheos Bakkikos* literally means "True Man True God". Orpheus was an earlier prototype of Christ that existed in Greek mythology. He was the son of Oeagrus, the king of Thrace, and the Muse Calliope. Apollo favored Orpheus and blessed him with many talents. He also gave him a lyre with seven strings.

It was said that Orpheus played the lyre with such melodious and moving tunes that the rivers stopped flowing, trees ceased to rustle and the rocks followed him. He could also tame ferocious beasts. His voice was so gentle and beautiful that he could calm the waves or lull dragons to sleep. Orpheus is also said to have taught the mysteries of Eleusis after his own initiation into the mysteries of Osiris.

After participating in the search for the golden fleece with the Argonauts, Orpheus married a nymph who was bitten by a serpent and died. Overwhelmed with grief, he sought and gained permission from Zeus to bring her back to Earth from the underworld. Using his lyre, he calmed the wild beasts and furies of Hades, but he was warned not to look at his beloved until he reached the land of the living. Just before he reached the gates of the underworld, he looked back to be sure that his wife was following him. She vanished from his sight and never returned. Upon returning to the living, Orpheus remained faithful to his wife and spurned the love of all other women who tore him limb from limb.

This myth follows the pattern of Osiris who was also torn to pieces. It shows that the love of Orpheus transcended worldly love and that the creatures of Earth would ultimately reject him and his principles. The most important part of the myth is his lyre with seven strings. This illustrates the power of the septenary influence. He could literally control matter and sway the wild beasts.

In this respect, the Pleiades are concerned with the realm of consciousness in which the blueprints for creation take place. If we wanted to go and inspect the blueprints for the different aspects of Earth, we are advised to visit the Pleiades. A highly charged form of energy has been found to exist within the Pleiades constellation and is known as the Photon Belt. As our sun circles the Pleiades approximately every 24,000 years, we can only wonder what exact effect this photon belt has on our culture or the entities who claim to channel energy from this region. In any event, that location in our galaxy is inundated with light. In practical experience, you might find that the Pleiadians operate something along the lines of holography. This is like the principle by which Nikola Tesla thought out his projects in full detail before he committed them to written blueprints. He was always correct.

All of this information, in combination with the mythological aspects related in this book, indicates that Preston Nichols' experience in the Pleiades was not just a dream.

Chapter Forty — Lyra and Beyond

Perhaps only time or your own experiences will tell exactly what the truth is.

Although the Pleiades have been referred to as a blueprint room, there has been no mention of the architect. Perhaps that is a story for a different time, but we are offered a clue with the lyre of Orpheus. After Orpheus was torn apart and died, Zeus honored the requests of Apollo and the Muses by placing the lyre in the stars in memory of him and his works. Today that constellation is known as Lyra.

The archetype of Lyra is discussed in a book entitled *The Prism of Lyra*. According to this book and different legends, the humanoids that settled the Pleiades, Sirius, and Orion all originated from Lyra. It is thought of as a prism because after the Fall from the original time line, consciousness fragmented from pure light into the seven rays of light as distinguished in the colors of the rainbow. Lyra is thought of as the matrix from which light originated. This brings us to a new subject which should properly be dealt with as a separate endeavor: the study of light.

NOTE: Those who want to further study the archetypal implications of Lyra should read "The Prism of Lyra" by Lyssa Royal and Keith Priest.

Epilogue

This book began with the personal experiences of Preston Nichols. The purpose of relaying his information is not only to tell an interesting story but to bridge a gap in humanity's understanding of UFOs and their accompanying phenomena. The purpose of my personal story is to demonstrate the existence of unseen forces of consciousness working to enlighten mankind and how they enabled the telling of Preston's story to take place.

All of the books I have written with Preston Nichols are criticized by some for being disjointed, and this one will be no exception. Although I make every effort possible to communicate clearly, there is a reason why the pieces of the puzzle are never in perfect focus. We are writing about phenomena that transcends the third dimension. The phenomena is not part of this realm and the information does not come as easy as finding the maintenance manual for a motorcycle. Obviously, critics and everyone else (including myself) would like everything handed to them on a silver platter as far as transcending the third dimension.

My interest in saying all this is not to silence critics but to bring home a very important point. Spiritual evolution is hard work. It is not arrived at merely by reading books. Although books can be a boost, one has to put ideas in to practice in order to change conditions. Each person's path is a separate and individual journey. For those who are seeking their own path, clues have been included in this book as to how you might go about it. All you really have to do is consult your own intuition and follow the horizon of your own consciousness. If those words don't ring a bell then it isn't meant to be rung. In keeping with the above, I would like to end this work with the last words the Buddha was said to have spoken.

"Decay is inherent in all component things. Work out your salvation with diligence."

A
Antique Saucers
by Preston B. Nichols

The UFO I have described in the main section of this book is a very advanced form of flying saucer. It has the typical operating system found inside the spherical ships and some of the flying discs. It is a complete state-of-the-art virtual reality system. There are also other types of flying craft around that I will now discuss. Although I have labeled them "Antique Saucers", they are far ahead of mankind's popular technology.

The next level of technology down from the state-of-the-art UFO is the wedge shaped ship. This is similar to the more advanced craft in that it has input chairs for the occupants. There are anywhere from two to six input chairs depending upon the complexity of the craft. A major difference with this craft is that you can see a control panel of sorts. There are some knobs and buttons as well as video screens. I get the impression that one of the controls might be a startup button. The actual steering and navigation functions are still inputed by neurological means from the beings.

Rather than a crystal computer, the wedge ship has a more conventional style computer that uses a very advanced chip technology. This connects to equipment constructed in part from Earth materials such as silver, gold, platinum, iron, copper, and aluminium. You will also find alloys in the equipment that are literally impossible to find on Earth.

The wedge shaped ship has more normal looking technology than the advanced craft. It does however operate on the same principles of electrogravitation and reality manipulation in order to propel itself. The power is generated from some sort of radioactive pellet in the center of a crystal. The pellet has been identified as Element 115. I have heard multiple reports that the wedge ships have fusion or fission reactors. It depends on who you talk to. I have never seen one because it has to be taken apart to understand the exact nature of the reactor.

I believe there are separate weapons and communications systems in the wedge ship. The more advanced ships have these built into the other interfacing functions aboard the craft, all controlled through the operator.

The cigar shaped ships are likewise powered by Element 115 and use technology similar to ours except that they are somewhere between fifty to one hundred years ahead of us. They have one chair and a massive control panel for this ship. The systems are bigger and more diversified with most of the input coming from the control panel as opposed to beings in a chair. The cigar craft also uses an antigravity system and a generator.

The interesting point is that all the different saucers use the same frequency transform to generate their twisters and spinners (see Chapter Six for an explanation of these terms). In doing an electromagnetic signature analysis, I have not heard anything but one electromagnetic signature emanating from UFOs. Apparently, this one signature of 435 Mhz is universally used for the drives. If you know what to listen for in the radio bands, you can hear the signature and tell when a UFO is close by.

B
The Particle Accelerator
by Preston B. Nichols

NOTE: The information in this appendix originally appeared in the book "Pyramids of Montauk".

In the fall of 1993 a particle accelerator had been discovered as a result of me doing a video fly-by of Camp Hero. What appeared to be a large circle cut out of the foliage was identified as a particle accelerator by my friend Danny, a nuclear physicist. I was showing him overhead videos I'd taken of the base. He got excited and asked me to freeze the frame. He then pulled out a diagram of a particle accelerator, held it up to the screen and began to identify the various parts of a particle accelerator.

"Here is the beam line. Here is the maintenance port. Here is the cryogenics (the science that deals with the production of very low temperatures and their effect on the properties of matter) port. Down here is the particle injection point."

If one were to overlay Danny's particle accelerator diagram on my video screen, it would fit exactly where the Montauk circle appeared.

All of this sheds a new light on the Montauk Project. I began to research accordingly and studied particle accelerators. What I found was that a very large particle accelerator is used to feed smaller ones. I believe the larger one to be located at Brookhaven National Labs. Because of the energetic interactions that occur between the different accelerators, the smaller ones have to be located some distance from the main one. Montauk and the eastern end of Long Island were chosen as an ideal location for the smaller accelerators.

Next, I will explain how this system of particle accelerators works. If you are not technically minded, you might wish to skip the rest of this appendix.

The process begins with the injection of protons into the large accelerator. A proton is a positively charged particle within the nucleus of an atom. It is the antithesis of an electron. For the purposes of the accelerator, the protons were generated by stripping the electrons off of hydrogen atoms. First, they separated the light hydrogen from the heavy hydrogen. This gave them light hydrogen with no neutrons in the nucleus. It is then very easy to strip the electron off of the hydrogen atom and given it a positive charge. It would then be a proton. A proton stream was then injected into the large accelerator and the protons would begin to accelerate. The protons generated would expand and begin to take up more space until they became more and more virtual.

At the output point of the large accelerator, the protons were travelling at about $.5c$ (c = the speed of light, so $.5c$ is half the speed of light). From the output point, the protons were sent down a magnetically focused tunnel and injected into the accelerator ring on the Montauk base itself. It would then be further accelerated to the speed of light.

What you are doing at the speed of light is taking advantage of the Albert Einstein formula that says energy is equal to mass times the velocity of light squared ($e=mc^2$). The reason this is significant is that a particle at the speed of light is going to have a certain amount of energy based upon the mass/velocity relationship in Einstein's equation, the other form of which can be stated $e=mv^2$ where v stands for velocity. The maximum velocity is the speed of light so the maximum energy is where v is replaced by c.

Appendix B – The Particle Accelerator

The whole idea of a particle accelerator is that you are getting a unit of electromagnetic energy (a proton, which acts like a particle) to continually increase its velocity. As the particles are converted to the speed of light, vast amounts of energy are released because you are going from the real world to a totally imaginary world which could also be defined as mental energy.

As I continued to study the particle accelerator at Montauk with Dan, all sorts of alarm bells and light bulbs were set off in my head because it enabled me to explain a problem I'd been encountering for years. Whenever I asked different psychics to read how much power they had at Montauk, they would invariably come up with an astronomical amount: a million megawatts of energy. This didn't make any sense because if you're going to run an amplifier of one million megawatts, it will require at least two million megawatts of power. There isn't enough power on Long Island to run the thing.

When I communicated this to Dan, he had already explained to me what I have just relayed about the different particle accelerators attaining the speed of light. I then asked him how much energy one of these particle accelerators could produce upon attaining the speed of light. Dan then grabbed a chart which had a number of things on it including energy output in comparison to circular diameters of accelerators. We had already measured the Montauk circle as having a 625 foot diameter. Sure enough, on Dan's chart we found one of the entries to be 625 feet. Was that a mere coincidence?

We estimated the other items from the chart, including the diameter of the beam and the energy being put into it. Dan did some figuring and said that the particle accelerator at Montauk was equivalent to a hundred megaton nuclear device. He then went to another chart to find out what a hundred megatons converts to in terms of power. It equaled one million megawatts of power, the same amount different psychics had read.

I began to discover more about particle accelerators after my meeting with Dan. I came across a number of reports of very large power amplifiers being built for particle accelerators. They were designed to operate at 435 Megahertz which means they probably found their way out to Montauk. These power amplifiers were called klystrons and replaced the huge amplitrons used in the underground. This was obviously an engineering decision because two or three klystrons could do the work of 24 amplitrons. They are easier to power and act similarly to a magnetron except that they are linear with no orbit. (A magnetron is a microwave signal source similar to that in a microwave oven. It consists of a tube with an electron orbit that produces vast amounts of RF energy.) Klystrons consist of a tube of about 100 feet long and 20 feet in diameter and are essentially a high powered microwave amplifier that drives the particle beam accelerator.

In the particle beam amplifier (which is the same as saying particle beam accelerator), they use atomic particles like neutrons and protons instead of electrons (which are used in a magnetron or amplitron). The protons/neutrons are then focused into an orbit so that a resonant action occurs in the cavities of the accelerator. A cavity is a resonant space which is bounded by a reflective surface of RF energy such as a metal plate or shielded surface. It is physically resonant based upon the velocity, in this case the speed of light.

These neutrons/protons were specially grouped in their orbit so as to act like energy packets in a magnetron or amplitron (which both have orbiting electrons). As the particles in the particle accelerator were sent around the circle at Montauk, thus approaching the speed of light, the cavity would group with the atomic particles into energy packets. The cavity is then resonating with the energy from the particles. When the electron beam is accelerated further, it imparts energy into the cavities and that translates into output.

The particle accelerator already has a particle orbit. The trick is to somehow group the particles in terms of relativistic phase velocity. If this is done, as the particle beam is approaching the speed of light, you could then literally tap the energy out of the particle accelerator with a group of cavities just like in a magnetron.

Appendix B — The Particle Accelerator

Within the particle beam amplifier that includes the 625 foot diameter circle at Montauk, two sets of cavities are positioned at right angles to each other surrounding a circle. Using the output of about a 30 megawatt transmitter, you drive one group of cavities on one of the axis which we'll call the X axis. Just as in a regular amplitron, the input power groups the electron beam spinning around in the amplitron with one set of cavities. This is called slow wave structure (slow wave refers to particles travelling below the speed of light). In the particle beam amplifier, we're not dealing with slow wave but with light velocity wave structure. The input cavities then group the particle beam at about $.9c$.

As the particle is accelerated faster and reaches c, it is going to release all the energy. The energy will then be released upon the bunched particles and the Y cavity will then pick up the energy. It is positioned $90°$ away from the X cavity and conducts the energy in whatever manner has been set.

In order to output the energy from the particle amplifier, it would be normal to put it into wave guides and send it back to the radar tower. But, this won't work because with a million megawatts the wave guides would melt. Instead of taking the energy out of the particle beam amplifier as an energy beam, they allowed the particle beam amplifier to become the antenna. The E field antenna which coupled in with the Delta T antenna was actually the circle of the particle beam amplifier which has an output power of a million megawatts. This is definitely enough to bend space and time.

They constructed the output cavity to go to some sort of rectifier which I still don't fully understand at this point. Some of this energy was used to drive the Delta T antenna, the top tip of which is just below the center of the ground. The bottom tip is way below the center of the ground and under the particle accelerator. To power the X and Y coils of the Delta T, they tapped the particle accelerator just above the ground. They then drove the Z coil, possibly as a white noise source, from the particle accelerator in the main town of Montauk (the traffic circle in the center of town). It is my supposition that they may have gotten some of that energy accelerated to the speed of light. Since the output from the accelerator in town was not modulated, it would be white noise and would serve as the correlating signal for bending time (reference Chapter 12 of *The Montauk Project*).

Bending time is not the only use of the particle accelerator. It is also used today as a particle beam weapon. It is known that UFOs are sensitive to 435 Megahertz with a 20 Megahertz band width. This is accomplished by using one set of cavities to bunch the particle beam at 435 MH. Then they will used the particle beam port with reflective mirrors and magnetic focusing to launch this thing as a particle beam weapon. When they do this, they generate two interlacing helical beams, very similar to the caduceus function. By controlling the phasing beams, they can control how far out they'll travel and at some point a destructive interference will occur. The beams will destroy each and in turn create an interference which will generate a miniature black hole. Modulation is the key to getting through the shield of the UFO which has been well known since the days of the early Sage radar when they began shooting down UFOs.

Glossary

cycle — A unit of activity within a wave that continually repeats itself. A cycle will go up and down before it repeats itself. If you visualize ocean waves that are all uniform, the series of waves would be called the "wave". The one ocean wave that a surfer might ride would be a "cycle".

Delta T — Short for "Delta Time". Delta is used in science to indicate change, thus "Delta T" would indicate a change in time.

Delta T antenna — An octahedronal antenna structure that is designed to bend time. Visually, it looks like two pyramids base to base. By definition, it can actually facilitate shifting time zones. Two coils are placed vertically around the edges of the pyramid structure at 90° angles to one another. A third coil surrounds the base. Shifting time zones was accomplished by pulsing and powering the Delta T antenna, as is discussed in Chapter 12 of *The Montauk Project*. Even when the antenna is not powered, it has a subtle interdimensional effect on the nature of time.

"electromagnetic bottle" — This refers to a "bottle effect" that is created when a specific space is surrounded by an electromagnetic field. The specific space itself is the inside of the "bottle". The walls would be the electromagnetic field. When people or objects are within the specific space, they would be within an "electromagnetic bottle".

electromagnetic wave — When an electric charge occurs that oscillates (swings back and forth), a field around the charge is generated. This field is both electric and magnetic in nature. This field also oscillates which in turn propagates a wave through space. This wave is called an electromagnetic wave.

Eleusinian Mysteries — A mystery school in Greece that was a direct descendant of the Egyptian Isis cult. It taught the night side or feminine energies and was said to have been originally taught by Isis herself.

Elohim — Webster's defines this word as God although it is more properly used to refer to the first born of God: the angels. The word "El" means God and the Elohim are considered to be the Fallen Angels or the Elder Race that inspired the creation of mankind.

extraterrestrials — In its broadest sense, extraterrestrial refers to anything not from Terra (the Earth). This term is now commonly used in UFOlogy to refer to beings that utilize the genetics of humans or compromise them in other ways in order to serve their own evolutionary ends.

435 Mhz — *The following technical description of 435 Mhz has been offered to Preston Nichols by his Pleiadian contacts. It is included for technical people only.* The spinner base of our reality is the fabric of space-time oscillating at 435 Mhz. This relates to the diameter of the black hole at the center of our galaxy based upon cyclotronic (refers to particles going in circular orbit) resonance as the black hole spins based upon the size and speed at which it's rotating and the energies being pulled through it at the speed of light. What is generated is a third order differential equation (way to express Space and Time) with angular limits on the trigonometric part of the differential: the angular limits solve the equation when you put in info or 435 Mhz that rotates through ϖ. The ratio of the frequency to the angular momentum is ϖ over 2.

frequency — The number of waves or cycles per second.

hertz — (abbr Hz) This is simply one cycle of a wave. A wave consists of numerous cycles that are repetitions of one cycle. To be a bit more technical, hertz is the complete fluctuation of a wave from plus (the highest point) to minus (the lowest point). Five hertz would be five cycles per second.

Metatron — Metatron is defined as the prototype for the basic constituents or subparticles of matter. It also refers to the full light spiral of matter as opposed to the half light or dwindling spiral of matter. In other words, metatronic energy would be that which is ingested with the full light spectrum or expansive light from the first cause.

MHz — Megahertz, which are equivalent to 1,000,000 hertz.

Montauk Boys — Refers to teenage boys, predominantly of Aryan descent with blue eyes and blond hair, who were abducted for mind control experiments done at Camp Hero located at Montauk Point, New York. They were programmed with many different agendas, one of which was to execute a martial law dictatorship in the case of societal chaos.

The Montauk Chair — An elaborate and esoteric mind control device which consisted in part of a lounge chair with three sets of coils set up with a pyramid around it. The coils were sensors designed to pick up the thoughts of a human being sitting in the chair. The thoughts were then decoded by a computer and linked to a transmitter so that they could be sent out and received by unwitting recipients. For further information on this technology and how it was developed in order to manipulate time, read *The Montauk Project: Experiments in Time*.

MRI — Magnetic Resonance Imaging. A procedure whereby visual images of the insides of the human body are reproduced through the use of electromagnetic principles. This is commonly used by today's medical profession and is far more detailed than an X-ray.

oscillator — A device that establishes and maintains oscillations. To oscillate means to swing back and forth. In electronics, an oscillation refers to a regular variation between maximum and minimum values, such as current or voltage

phase — The time interval between when one thing occurs and the instant a second related thing takes place.

Philadelphia Experiment — A secret experiment conducted in 1943 at the Philadelphia Naval Yard wherein the *U.S.S. Eldridge* was outfitted with degaussing coils so that it would appear invisible to radar. According to witnesses, it disappeared completely and teleported to the Virginia coast.

Psi Corp — A secret arm of the U.S. intelligence community consisting of trained psychics who indulge in almost every type of psychic activity one can imagine. A small sampling of their activities includes the following: remote viewing, controlling people through their dreams, targeting a person with intent to harm, and the use of telepathy to determine the actions of a war enemy.

psycho-active — This pertains to any activity or function that has an affect on the mind or psyche. In this book, psycho-active refers primarily to electromagnetic functions or electronic equipment that influence human thinking and behavior.

psychotronics — The science and discipline of how life functions. It includes the study of how technology interacts with the human mind, spirit and body. Science, mathematics, philosophy, metaphysics and esoteric studies are united through the study of psychotronics. It would also include other realities and how we interface with other dimensions of existence.

pulse modulations — These are sent as a series of short pulses which are separated by relatively long stretches of time with no signal being transmitted.

RF — Radio Frequency. Frequencies above 20,000 hertz are called radio frequencies because they are useful in radio transmissions.

radio wave — An electromagnetic wave that carries intelligent information (pictures, sound, etc).

relativistic — Relativistic functions refer to activities that are out of our normal reference frame. It also concerns how activities in other reference frames relate to ours. Relativity embraces the concept of everything without any limitations, including other dimensions and the entire universe(s).

scry — The ancient art of looking into a crystal and foretelling potentialities was called scrying. It refers to any activity where one is peering past a veil and seeing the truth.

sideband — This is the component of radio waves that actually carries the intelligent information.

soloton — A self contained electromagnetic field. It does not spread out in linear fashion but goes to a boundary and then stops.

space-time — When you study higher level physics, it becomes apparent that space and time are inextricably related to each other. It is considered less accurate to refer to just space or time by itself (because they don't exist by themselves). That would be like saying your mouth ate the dinner.

torus — A doughnut shape. According to physicists and esotericists, the universe is shaped in the form of a torus.

transceiver — An instrument that serves as both a receiver and a transmitter.

transmitter — A device or unit that sends a signal or message.

transponder — A transceiver that automatically transmits electrical signals when actuated by a specific signal.

ultraterrestrial — refers to a higher order being who can function within the Metatronic or full light spiral. They do not vampirize or compromise human beings but work according to a divine plan.

wave — A state of motion that rises and falls periodically is called a wave. It can be transmitted from one particular area to another with no actual transport of matter taking place. A wave consists of many cycles and can carry signals, pictures or sounds.

Bibliography

Blavatasky, H.P. *The Secret Doctrine*, Volumes I & II
The Theosophy Company, Los Angeles, California

Campbell, Joseph *The Masks of God: Creative Mythology*
The Viking Press, Larousse, New York ©1968

Countryman, J. *Atlantis and the Seven Stars*
St. Martin's Press, New York ©1979

Fortune, Dion *The Mystical Qabalah*
Samuel Weiser, York Beach, Maine

Grant, Michael *Roman Myths*
Charles Scribner's Sons, New York, ©1971

Grant, Kenneth *Aleister Crowley and the Hidden God*
Skoob Books Publishing, London ©1992

Grant, Kenneth *Cults of the Shadow*
Skoob Books Publishing, London ©1994

Grant, Kenneth *The Magical Revival*
Skoob Books Publishing, London ©1991

Graves, Robert *The Greek Myths*
Moyer Bell Ltd, Mount Kisco, New York ©1960

Owen, Lara *Her Blood is Gold*
Harper Collins, New York ©1993

Reed, A.W. *Myths & Legends of Australia*
Taplinger Publishing Company, New York ©1965

Schmidt, Joñl *Greek and Roman Mythology*
MacGraw-Hill Book Co., New York ©1980

The Montauk Project
EXPERIMENTS IN TIME

SILVER ANNIVERSARY EDITION

A BRAND NEW VERSION

ISBN 978-1-937859-21-3 $25.00

The Montauk Project was originally released in 1992, causing an uproar and shocking the scientific, academic, and journalistic communities, all of whom were very slow to catch on to the secret world that lurks beyond the superficial veneer of American civilization.

A colloquial name for secret experiments that took place at Montauk Point's Camp Hero, the Montauk Project represented the apex of extensive research carried on after World War II; and, in particular, as a result of the phenomena encountered during the Philadelphia Experiment of 1943 when the United States Navy attempted to achieve radar invisibility.

The Montauk Project attempted to study why and how human beings, when exposed to high powered electromagnetic waves, suffered mental disorientation, physical dissolution or even death. A further ramification of this phenomena is that such electromagnetic waves rescrambled components of the material universe itself. According to reports, this research not only included successful attempts to manipulate matter and energy but also time itself.

It has now been over twenty-five years since *The Montauk Project* originally appeared in print. In this *Silver Anniversary Edition*, you will not only read the original text, accompanied by commentary which includes details that could not be published at the original time of publication, but also an extensive summary of a twenty-five year investigation of the Montauk Project which culminated in actual scientific proof of time travel capabilities.

ORDER TODAY FROM SKY BOOKS
AT OUR BOOK STORE: www.skybookusa.com

THE SEQUELS

The stir and controversy produced by **The Montauk Project** was overwhelming to the society it was released into in 1992. The powers that be behind the military industrial complex had a lot to explain. A whole new genre of television shows were spawned in an attempt to absorb the fallout of questions and to do damage control on the trail of information thus exposed. In the meantime, Peter Moon set about trying to verify the Montauk Project and the result was of the first sequel to this amazing series:

Montauk Revisited: Adventures in Synchronicity
BY PRESTON NICHOLS AND PETER MOON
This sequel pursues the mysteries of time brought to light in **The Montauk Project** and unmasks the occult forces behind the science and technology used in the Montauk Project. An ornate tapestry is revealed which interweaves the mysterious associations of the Cameron clan with the genesis of American rocketry and the magick of Aleister Crowley and Jack Parsons. **Montauk Revisited** continues the Montauk investigation and unleashes incredible new characters and information.
ISBN 0-9631889-1-7, 249 pages, illustrations, and photos...................$22.00

After **Montauk Revisited** was completed, and much to his surprise, Peter Moon discovered that the mysterious trail of synchronicities led to the revelation that the site of "The Montauk Project" experiments was sacred Native American ground that was once accompanied by ancient pyramids which could be clearly seen in old photographs of Montauk. The result of this brand new investigation was:

Pyramids of Montauk: Explorations in Consciousness
BY PRESTON NICHOLS AND PETER MOON
This astonishing second sequel to **The Montauk Project** and **Montauk Revisited** awakens the consciousness of humanity to its ancient history and origins through the discovery of pyramids at Montauk. A full examination of the mysteries of the pyramids at Montauk Point reveals that the Montauk Tribe were the royal family of Long Island and that they used the name Pharaoh as a designation that connected their heritage to ancient Egypt and beyond. The discovery that these pyramids were placed on sacred native American ground opens the door to an unprecedented investigation of the mystery schools of earth and their connection to Egypt, Atlantis, Mars and the star Sirius. This book explains why Montauk was chosen as a select location for pyramids and time travel experimentation. **The Pyramids of Montauk** stirs the quest for the end of time as we know it.
ISBN 0-9631889-2-5, 256 pages, illustrations, photos........................$22.00

After **Encounter in the Pleiades** was published, Peter Moon had accumulated information connecting Montauk to Tibet. Peter's research culminated with a visit from world-renown German author, Jan van Helsing, who shared his photos of the mysterious German flying craft as discussed in:

The Black Sun: Montauk's Nazi- Tibetan Connection
BY PETER MOON

After World War II, Allied military commanders were stunned to learn the depth of the Nazi regime's state secrets which included the world's best intelligence organization with meticulous research files on secret societies, eugenics and other scientific pursuits that boggled the imagination of the Allied command. Even more spectacular was an entire web of underground rocket and flying saucer factories with accompanying technology that still defies ordinary beliefs. A missing U-boat fleet possessing the most advanced submarine technology in the world left many wondering if the Nazis had escaped with yet more secrets or even with Hitler himself. Behind these mysteries was an even deeper element: a secret order known to initiates as the Order of the Black Sun, an organization so feared that it became illegal to even print their symbols and insignia in modern Germany. The Black Sun probes deep into these strange associations and their connection to Montauk Point where an American military facility was used by the Nazis to further their own strange experiments and continue the hidden agenda of the Third Reich.
ISBN 0-9631889-4-1, 304 pages, with photos, illustrations.....$24.95

The Black Sun was followed by a series of books, the first about Preston's intriguing involvement as a sound engineer for many popular music groups of the '60s and '70s as well as a UFO legal case on Long Island.

The Music of Time
BY PRESTON NICHOLS & PETER MOON

This book blends music with time travel as Preston Nichols reveals his hidden role as an expert sound engineer who recorded hundreds of hit records during the Golden Era of Rock 'n Roll. For the first time, Preston reveals his employment at Brookhaven Labs and how his connections in the music industry were used for mind control and manipulation of the masses. Ultimately, Preston's adventures lead to his association with John Ford, the founder of the Long Island UFO Network, who was arrested and railroaded into jail without a trial and is still locked up to this day.
ISBN 0-9678162-0-3, 244 pages................................$24.95

SYNCHRONICITY & THE SEVENTH SEAL

Peter Moon's consummate work on Synchronicity begins with a layman's scientific description of the quantum mechanics of the universe and how the observer or spirit experiences the principle of synchronicity as a divine expression of the infinite mind.

Besides exploring parallel universes, numerous personal experiences of the author are included which not only forges a pathway of how to experience and appreciate synchronicity, but it goes very deep into the magical exploits of intriguing characters who sought to tap the ultimate powers of creation. This not only includes the most in depth analysis and accurate depiction of the Babalon Working in print but also various antics and breakthroughs of the various players and that which influenced them. These characters include the legacies and personas of Jack Parsons, Marjorie Cameron, L. Ron Hubbard and Aleister Crowley.

Peter Moon adds exponential intrigue to the mix by telling us of his personal experiences with these people and their wake which leads to even deeper encounters which penetrates the mysterious legacy of John Dee. This pursuit of synchronicities leads Peter Moon to an captivating encounter with Joseph Matheny who had similar experiences to Peter but has his own version of a space-time project known as Ong's Hat. Matheny's incredible synchronicities led him to create one of the highest forms of artificial intelligence known to man, a computer known as the Metamachine designed to precipitate and generate synchronicities. These synchronicities lead to the book's climax, a revelation of the true Seventh Seal. The proof is delivered with no counter claims ever having been made. You can make up your own mind.
455 pages, ISBN 0-9678162-7-0..$29.95

The Montauk Book of the Dead — BY PETER MOON
A tale of the intrigue and power which hovers over the most sacred kernel of our existence: the secrets of life and death. This personal story of Peter Moon pierces the mystery of death and reveals fascinating details of his years aboard L. Ron Hubbard's mystery ship but gives the most candid and inside look ever at one of the most controversial figures in recent history.
The book covers the all out war which was waged by governmental forces and spy agencies to obtain the legally construed rights to the above mentioned work and all of the developments and techniques that ensued from it.
ISBN 978-0-9678162-3-4, 451 pages..$29.95

Montauk Book of the Living — BY PETER MOON
The discovery of a mysterious quantum relic tied to the Montauk Pharoahs opens the door to understanding the greatest mysteries of history including the biological truth behind the Virgin Birth and how this theme intertwines with the descendants of these Amazons who live today and are known as the Blue People of the Sahara. Other occult surprises include new revelations concerning Aleister Crowley's The Book of the Law and demonstrates that the ancients who built the pyramids knew deeper secrets concerning DNA than our scientists of today.
ISBN 978-0-9678162-6-5, 384 pages..$29.95

SPANDAU MYSTERY · BY PETER MOON
Much intrigue at the end of World War II centered around the secret projects sponsored by Rudolph Hess such as the Antarctic project but the construction of Vril flying saucers. These tasks eventually crossed the path of General George S. Patton whose job was to recover the secret technology of the Germans and safeguard it for American use. After accomplishing his mission and compiling a German history of the war, General Patton was killed in a dubious accident, the mystery of which has never been solved and has been magnified by government refusal to declassify the file on the investigation of his death. This story explores the intertwining lives of Patton and Hess who was suspiciously killed just before his imminent release.
350+ pages, ISBN 978-0-9678162-4-1..$22.00

FOR MORE BOOKS VISIT *WWW.SKYBOOKSUSA.COM*

Coming in 2021
The Roswell Deception and Demystification of World War II
by Douglas Dietrich with Peter Moon

With illustrations and actual photos, you will learn the verifiable and actual history of the enormous and very effective Japanese super-sized dirigibles and balloon bombs that were made for both biological and conventional war and how they used these to coerce the Allies so as to secure an economic victory for Japan that is still in force to this day.

The Roswell Deception is genuine history that the Government has classified in order to hide the lies and crimes of key people and those who continue their legacy. This includes the social engineering of what really happened at Roswell and the steering of people's minds to believe in aliens.

Did you ever wonder why the Japanese have such a great economy while the U.S. faltered? Containing pivotal truths that can neither be denied nor ignored, this book will cause historians to change their narratives.

ISBN 978-1-937859-23-7, 308 pages, photos, illustrations...$24.95

The Transylvanian Series

TRANSYLVANIAN SUNRISE is the story of an unprecedented archeological discovery beneath the Romanian Sphinx in the Bucegi Mountains. Radu Cinamar visits this secret site where he witnessed a holographic Hall of Records left by an advanced civilization and three mysterious tunnels leading deep into the bowels of the Inner Earth. *Transylvanian Sunrise* chronicles the political intrigue surrounding the discovery of these artifacts which represents the dawn of a new era for Mankind.
288 pages, ISBN 978-0-9678162-5-8...$29.95

TRANSYLVANIAN MOONRISE corroborates Radu's story with newspaper articles as he is sought out by a mysterious Tibetan Lama who takes Radu on a mystical journey to Tibet where he receives a secret initiation and a sacred manuscript from the blue goddess Machandi. This is an initiation of the highest order that will take you far beyond your ordinary imagination in order to describe events that have molded the past and will influence the future in the decades ahead.
288 pages, ISBN 978-0-9678162-8-9...$29.95

MYSTERY OF EGYPT features an expedition to explore the First Tunnel in the holographic chamber: the one to Egypt. Ancient artifacts are discovered which tell the history of the Earth in holographic form, the most controversial of which include remarkable adventure that includes explorations in time to the First Century A.D. This book also includes updates from Cezar since their last meeting.
240 pages, ISBN 978-1-937859-08-4...$29.95

THE SECRET PARCHMENT — FIVE TIBETAN INITIATION TECHNIQUES presents invaluable techniques for spiritual advancement that came to Radu Cinamar in the form of an ancient manuscript whose presence in the world ignited a series of quantum events, extending from Jupiter's moon Europa and reaching all the way to Antarctica, Mount McKinley and Transylvania. An ancient Romanian legend comes alive as a passage way of solid gold tunnels, extending miles in the Transylvanian underground is revealed to facilitate super-consciousness as well as lead to the nexus of Inner Earth where "All the Worlds Unite."
288 pages, ISBN 978-0-9678162-5-8...$29.95

THE WHITE BAT — THE ALCHEMY OF WRITING
Told in a personal narrative, Peter Moon relates how he was being drawn to Transylvania via the dream of a white bat, long before he became involved with Montauk, only discover that there are actual white bats in Transylvania that are unknown to science. This book synthesizes the dream process with the creative process and teaches you to do the same.
288 pages, ISBN 978-1-937859-15-2...$22.00

INSIDE THE EARTH
THE SECOND TUNNEL

Stories of the Inner Earth have both fascinated and perplexed mankind since the dawn of time. Now, for the first time, hard scientific data is provided that the Earth's core is not what conventional science has always assumed.

More amazing than the science, however, are the personal adventures of Radu Cinamar whose position in Department Zero, Romania's secretive intelligence division, allows him to penetrate ancient subterranean passage ways and meet citizens of civilizations in the Inner Earth.

Familiar characters from the ***Transylvania Series*** also reappear, including the enigmatic Tibetan lama, Repa Sundhi, also known as Dr. Xien, who states:

> "If someone had a device or machine that could start up and go everywhere they want, especially towards the center of the Earth, the machine would be blocked and stop at a certain point because of the frequency of vibration to be found there. Just how far you can go with such a machine can be limited by reason of your own consciousness which can in and of itself restrict the dimensional range of such a device or the extent to which it can penetrate other realms. This applies to both human beings as well as material objects. Your ability to access such a region is determined by what your own individual consciousness can or will allow you to experience."

In this exhilarating description of mysteries inside the Earth, Radu Cinamar presents a unique way to penetrate the Inner Earth through the process of feeling and the effects that will develop from such an experience. To enhance the reader's understanding of this very guarded subject, ***Inside the Earth — The Second Tunnel*** includes multiple illustrations that include depictions of Inner Earth geography.

Within the core of the Earth is intelligence reaching far beyond the scope of ordinary human consciousness. Inside the Earth is an opportunity for initiation as you explore the frequencies of your own inner nature.

240 pages, ISBN 978-1-937859-20-6...$22.00

FORGOTTEN GENESIS

FORGOTTEN GENESIS delves into ancient history in a way that no book has done before, explaining and illustrating changes in DNA that have taken place over millennia and how Mankind has evolved into what it is today. Some of the "hot spots" of human history, which have either remained unknown or have only been considered from mythological positions, are explained, including: Atlantis, Troy, Shambhala, and Hyperborea. The diversity and the accuracy of the explanations presented are clear and conclusive, combining pure esoteric knowledge with certain scientific elements. Particular emphasis is placed upon the existence and manifestation of inter-dimensional chasms or portals at the "intersections" between the physical plane and the etheric plane.

FROM THE AUTHOR:

"Even though the notions presented in this book are delicate, I considered it necessary to take a step forward and expose some deeper aspects. I also believe that the elements presented in the other volumes of this series have prepared the ground for the interested reader to gain a fair understanding of the esoteric and other factors involved with this fascinating and complex scenario. I will continue with this more elaborate approach which has become a necessity in the current context of the times. I hope that the readers of this series of volumes will correctly understand my approach and the sincere desire to expose to the world some unknown aspects of the reality we live in."

— *Radu Cinamar*

THE MONTAUK PULSE

The Montauk Pulse originally went into print in the winter of 1993 to chronicle the events and discoveries regarding the ongoing investigation of the Montauk Project by Preston Nichols and Peter Moon. It has remained in print and been issued quarterly ever since. With a minimum of six pages and a distinct identity of its own, the Pulse has expanded to not only chronicle the developments concerning the Montauk investigation, but has expanded to include all the adventures that have surrounded Peter Moon since that time. This includes his adventures with David Anderson and the groundbreaking events that are occurring in Romania. For regular updates, subscribe to the *Montauk Pulse* newsletter. Subscribing to the *Pulse* directly contributes to the efforts of the author in writing more books and chronicling the effort to understand time and all of its components. Past support has been crucial to what has developed thus far. We appreciate your support in helping to unravel various mysteries of Earth-based and non-Earth-based consciousness. It makes a difference. You can subscribe for $20.00 annually if you are in the U.S.A. or $30.00 if you are overseas. See the order form on the back of this page.

The Time Travel Education Center

The Time Travel Education Center was created in 2015 in order to educate the public on the simple math and science behind the concept of time travel (with free videos) and also to keep people informed on related aspects to this very avant-garde and rarified subject. The science and math, based upon the genius of Dr. David Anderson, are introduced at an eighth grade level of mathematics yet the concepts are astonishingly profound.

Peter Moon has also prepared an on-going video series on the Psychology of Space-Time in order to help people understand the issues surrounding this phenomenal technology and why it is not readily available for everyone. There will be further videos as time allows.

You can become a free member of The Time Travel Education Center by going to the website below, and you can also become a paid subscriber which will give you access to further information including books in progress by Peter Moon. Your support is important.

VISIT THE TIME TRAVEL RESEARCH CENTER:

www.timetraveleducationcenter.com

Sky Books — ORDER FORM

We wait for ALL checks to clear before shipping. This includes Priority Mail orders. If you want to speed delivery time, please send a U.S. Money Order or use MasterCard or Visa. Those orders will be shipped right away. Complete this order form and send with payment or credit card information to:
Sky Books, Box 769, Westbury, New York 11590-0104

Name	
Address	
City	
State / Country	Zip
Daytime Phone (In case we have a question) ( )	

☐ This is my first order ☐ I have ordered before ☐ This is a new address

Method of Payment: ☐ Visa ☐ MasterCard ☐ Money Order ☐ Check

\# ___ — ___ — ___ — ___

Expiration Date ___ Signature ___

TITLE	QTY	PRICE
The Montauk Pulse (1 year - free shipping US orders)...$20.00		
The Montauk Pulse (international - free shipping)...$30.00		
Montauk Project SILVER ANNIVERSARY EDITION...$25.00		
Note: There is no additonal shipping for the Montauk Pulse. International subscription is $30.00. **Subtotal**		
For delivery in NY add 8.63% tax		
U.S. Shipping: $6.00 for 1st book plus $1.50 for 2nd, etc.		
Foreign shipping: (email us first at skybooks@yahoo.com)		
Total		

FOR MORE BOOKS VISIT WWW.SKYBOOKSUSA.COM

www.ingramcontent.com/pod-product-compliance
Lightning Source LLC
Chambersburg PA
CBHW070052080526
44586CB00013B/1027